The B-Side of Paradise

Alfred D'Alessandro

THE B-SIDE OF PARADISE

What To Do Media

ISBN 979-8-9913525-0-5 (pbk)
ISBN 979-8-9913525-1-2 (d)
ISBN 979-8-9913525-2-9 (hc)

Cover Design by MUTI
Interior Book Design by *the*BookDesigners
Edited by Julie Blattberg

This is a memoir about real events in my life. Although it was all a long time ago and my memory is not as good as it once was. Just in case some of it may be complete fabrications, I have changed everyone's names. With two exceptions: Princeton President Bill Bowen—because everyone loved him. And, of course, my name. Because this is a memoir.

Table of Contents

The Beginning

My Best-Fit College Trip to Nowhere

When my son Beckett was seventeen, I took him to see a college counselor who told us that for an extortionate fee he could help him navigate the college applications process. Even more alarming than his price was the way he insisted on calling his methodology "a rational approach to finding your best-fit school."

There's a little round man in my head who laughs whenever people say things like "the milk of human kindness," "world peace," or "rational approach to finding your best-fit school." The truth is, I have never been convinced college selection is the kind of thing that lends itself to logic and analytical thinking. In any case, if such a thing is humanly possible, I would like to see it, because there were no signs of intelligent life in my dog's breakfast of a college search.

That said, I forked over a small fortune for Beckett's counseling because I am equally unconvinced that college planning should be left in the hands of a teenager. Or the teenager's parents. Let me explain...

The B-Side of Paradise

My gloriously ill-fated, Ivy League career began in the spring of my junior year in the boy's locker room of Long Island's Baytown High School. More specifically on the frosted-glass window of its hydrotherapy room across from the showers.

Walking past, I heard the whir and tick of a 16-millimeter projector inside. Someone was watching game film of our past football season, and I stopped to follow the action from the other side of the glass. In one of those great coincidences in life, there I was: all six inches of me running for glory in our championship game.

While it was always nice to watch myself do things, I wondered why anybody would hole themselves up on such a beautiful day in that dreadful little room. Barren as it was, but for the 150-gallon stainless-steel hydrotherapy tub, a folding chair, and a ball of bloodied ankle tape in the corner. There was always a ball of bloodied ankle tape in the corner.

Naturally, I was curious to know who might be in there. It was too early, after all, for the coaches to start prepping for the fall season. And I heard none of the raucous animal sounds one might expect if my teammates were gathered inside for an encore screening of our team's crowning achievement, Baytown High's first Long Island football title.

When the play was over, the film cryptically cut away to our second game of the season against our archrivals from Farmingdale. There I was in the spotlight again. This time, wearing white and making a defensive play in front of a packed Baytown home field crowd. The two plays lasted little more than ten seconds. And when they were over, they began again.

For some reason, someone had made a little movie about me. And it was streaming, like it had a mind of its own, across that frosted glass in a continuous loop. Cupping my ear to the door, I listened for a distinguishing sound that might reveal who was on the other side. But there was only the sad whir and jacked up *tick, tick, tick* of the projector. As if that old Bell + Howell was screening my life for no one in an empty room.

Being young and naïve, and despite my surprisingly strong academic record kind of stupid—I had a strange feeling that someone—or something—knew I was going to be there at that exact moment...and was trying to send me a message. I got this gauzy out-of-body feeling that, as someone who had grown up watching first-run episodes of *The Twilight Zone*, I associated with the late, great Rod Serling. From there, my imagination ran wild.

One unearthly thought led to another, and I questioned, in my altered state of teenage stupor, if it all might be a mental projection. Like I was watching myself watch a movie about me projected from memories in my own mind.

"Whoa!"

On *The Twilight Zone*, spectral images of a character's past often signified a transformation. Sure enough, those ten seconds of my life caught on film were about to change everything for me. Though I didn't know it at the time, this was my first encounter with *The B-Side of Paradise*.

You see, any of the other 100-plus players on the varsity and J.V. teams, the water boys, the cheerleaders, that half of Baytown who always seemed to know everyone else's business, even the custodial crew whose job it was to pick up the ball of bloodied ankle tape in the corner would have known that a college recruiter was inside watching my highlight reel.

It was common knowledge to everyone but me, it seems, that NCAA scouts had descended on our school in droves after we won the Long Island Division 1 championship the past fall. Although I was one of a relatively small group of players receiving their attention, I had no idea any of it was going on.

The next morning, about when I thought odd interdimensional things had stopped happening, Baytown High's guidance counselor, Miss Brooks, summoned me to her office. Only then did I come to understand that the phantom in the hydro room was a Princeton University football recruiter.

"How would you like to go to Princeton?" she asked, as if that was something I might have been thinking about. "I just got off the phone with their admissions office," she told me. "They said, 'Al D'Alessandro would be'" (wait for it) "'a good fit at Princeton.'" Then she looked at me as if I might have something to add to the conversation.

But I hadn't given college much thought until then. Consumed as I was with the more important concerns of a high school junior, such as girls and beer parties in the woods.

Nor did the topic get much airtime at family dinners. That were one non-stop lecture about how my sister was going to get a reputation if she didn't stop hanging out in her greaser friends' muscle cars. Which usually ended with her in tears despite my parent's assurances that they were just telling her for her own good

Come to think of it, the only college talk I had ever been privy to before my meeting with Miss Brooks was the night my dad bragged to some cocktail party drunk that I was going to go to Harvard someday. But I was nine and I think he only said it because the guy kept spilling his whiskey sour on our carpet, and he was trying to get him to leave.

That said, I wasn't living under a rock. I knew the Ivy League was a good thing. And Miss Brooks, hot to catch just her third Princeton Tiger by the tail since Baytown's founding in 1956, was sending strong signals for me to get on board. Then she gave me the crooked eyebrow and ended the meeting on a bit of a down note when she insisted, "But you have to get your board scores up."

Anyway, I just said, "Cool." And she was cool with that.

My Dog's Breakfast Is Served

When I got home that afternoon, just to confuse matters, I had mail from Brown University and Columbia, who, judging by the text of their letters, thought I would be a "good fit" at their schools, too. I began to wonder if these people were doing any background checks, seeing that I was well known at Baytown for being a bit of a cut up. At times trying the patience of the very people whose favorable opinion I might need for a college recommendation.

Like when I got Old Jenkovitz so worked up he told me he would kick my ass out of Honors Social Studies in a heartbeat except my essays were the best in the class. I wasn't always proud of my behavior. But somebody had to disrupt the New York State public school curriculum. It wasn't my fault it always had to be me.

It all got me thinking that Miss Brooks should know about Jenks, that old skeleton of a Civics teacher—who in my darkest dreams I thought could bury me along with her plans. So, I dropped by to see her the next day and she assured me that, "Mr. Jenkovitz thinks very highly of you." That's when I knew Miss Brooks was running an operation around me and everybody was going to play ball. Finally, when she didn't say boo about Brown or Columbia, I left her office thinking Princeton was my destiny.

Alas, there's always a twist. And the odd turn to my rational approach to college selection came the next day. When I received three more "good fit" letters, this time from scholarship schools. Each of them included family invitations to their upcoming prospect weekends. The first was the University of Maryland, whose team mascot, I discovered, is a turtle. So, I put them at the bottom of my good-fit college list.

But it was what came next that threatened to foil Miss Brooks' devious scheme: one of those "you can't make this stuff up" moments in life, in which I opened my envelopes from Rice and Purdue. The enigmatic appellations that captured my imagination the first time I saw them scroll across the halftime report of the College Football Game of the Week when I was seven years old. And a swell of wonder from childhood came flashing back to me.

Amongst all the colleges named after their geographic locations, like Georgia Tech and Michigan State, there was something exotic about the sight and sound of the words Rice and Purdue. Who even knew where they were? On distant mountaintops? Hidden behind moated castle walls? Peeking out through low hanging clouds in some undiscovered part of America?

I imagined that I would need a secret password to get past their gates like Groucho Marx in *Horse Feathers* when he had to say "swordfish" to recruit ringers at a speakeasy for Huxley College's big game against Darwin. Somehow, in my child's mind, Huxley's antic world of robes, mortarboards, and leather helmets put a face to the names of these mythical sounding bastions of higher education and any romantic notions I harbored about college life after that became tied to them.

When I wrapped my eyes around Purdue's medieval griffin and Rice's Athenian owl proudly embossed on their letterheads, it felt like the moment had been preordained. "Miss Brooks or no Miss Brooks," I thought, "I'm going to the mountain top to see them."

Enter the teenager's parents, or, more precisely, my dad, who could take the romance out of anything or anyone. When I told him the news, he said, faster than the college football scores scrolled across our black-and-white television screen, "Rice and Purdue are too far to drive; we can go to Maryland."

There it was. The deadly Too-Far-to-Drive Card. The scourge of rational college decision-making itself. I don't know how I didn't see it coming, because it was just like my dad to play it. And there was little I could do when he pulled out that childhood-fantasy assassin Too-Far-to-Drive Card and slammed it down onto the gameboard of my life except cross two schools off my good-fit college list. And that's exactly what I did.

The Book of Unfinished Journeys

So, we piled into the car: mom in the navigator seat with the Rand McNally Large Scale Road Atlas of the Mid-Atlantic States and headed to College Park, home to the highly regarded University of Maryland, that by virtue of its geographic desirability had just risen two notches up my newly shortened list of good-fit schools.

On the way down, my dad worked the radio dial like a pro. Switching channels at the first sign of static as we moved out of range on the New York, the New Jersey, and

finally the Delaware stations, always in search of the senti-
mental trombone sounds of Tommy Dorsey or the clarinet
improvisations of Artie Shaw.

Sometimes the New Jersey Turnpike can drive me crazy.
And not just because it doesn't have any scenery. No, the New
Jersey Turnpike could make me go tilt because it reminded me of the Great Atlantic City Turnaround. Our family's
infamous vacation on the Jersey Shore—the one where my
mother, my sister, and I spent the better part of a day making
sandwiches to fill the Coleman family-sized cooler for our
beach week ahead.

Early the next morning, we packed the trunk of our new
Ford Galaxy and in the space of ten hours drove down to the
Jersey shore, turned around, and retraced our steps back to
Baytown when we couldn't find a vacant room anywhere in
the city.

My dad went to work the next day while the rest of us
made daily trips to Jones Beach from our home barely fifteen
minutes away until all the sandwiches were gone. Then our
vacation was over. The last one, as it turned out, our family
would ever take.

Aborted missions were something of an avocation for
my dad. Each of them carefully catalogued in the alma-
nac-style family history in my mind, such as our trip to the
Polo Grounds to see Willie Mays play the Mets that ended
on the Triboro Bridge when my dad's aging Oldsmobile, that
he mentioned had been running hot for a few days, began to
overheat.

When we got home, about when Willie was running out
to center field for the third inning in Washington Heights,
my mother didn't need to see the white vapor spewing from
that Old 88's hood or catch a whiff of the sickly sweet smell

of burning radiator fluid to know what had happened. "I told you to take the new car. What did you expect?" Our road trip to Maryland, however, would instantly become the master work in the *Anthology of D'Alessandro Family Unfinished Journeys.*

The ACC Abortion

The credits for the screen adaptation in my mind of the *ACC Abortion* begin to roll as we exit MD193 West onto Paint Branch Drive in College Park. Approaching the university gates, we were roundly welcomed by a complete absence of human activity, like we were late for some kind of evacuation.

It being the end of the school year, we understood there wouldn't be many students around. But on this day, the University of Maryland's campus was a ghost town. There were no guards at the security gate. No landscaping crews on the campus lawns. And no welcoming sign, "The Honorable Alfred D'Alessandro Sr., Right This Way."

Inside the main entrance, my father pulled the car to the side of the road and turned off the radio. Which was never a good sign. Looking straight ahead with his hands in the ten and two positions on the steering wheel, he delivered the death knell for our campus-recruiting visit. "There's nothing here," he said.

My father had a way of delivering a declarative statement with such finality it could defy logic. Clearly there was an entire college campus spread out before us, complete with red-brick Georgian-style buildings with white columns, one of those bronze college plaques that read "University of Maryland Founded in 1856," and a field of red flowers in the shape of the letter M on the front lawn. Even against all this evidence, a simple "there's nothing here" from my dad could create doubt in your mind.

In the front seat, my folks squabbled over whose responsibility it was to find out where we were supposed to meet the coach. My father said it was *mine*. My mother reminded him that *he* was the adult. *I* suggested we drive onto campus until we see a sign for the athletic center and then *follow it*. It was hard to tell if my father gave my idea the consideration I thought it deserved. But it certainly didn't change his mind.

"Nah," he said, "there's nothing here." And then with the camera pulling back into a long shot, he put the car in drive and methodically executed a three-point turn: the most traumatic vehicular maneuver under five miles per hour of my life. Finally, with the proud white columns and majestic portico of McKeldin Library now in our rearview mirror, he gave it the gas and we headed home.

What *was* he thinking?

Only with this writing, almost half a century later, did it occur to me that he might not have appreciated the historic significance of the giant graffiti that greeted us at the entrance. Specifically, the part that read "Out of Vietnam Now!" A plausible if not obvious explanation that I may have suppressed all these years due to its disturbing connection to the Night of the Flying Christmas Cannoli, that memorable holiday evening when I learned the hard way that my father never met a war he didn't like. Except, of course, the one he was in.

Knowing my dad's ambivalence for his own military service, I felt comfortable sharing my feelings with him about the armed forces that evening. Perhaps I was too direct in expressing my thoughts about the conflict overseas that was the topic of much discussion at the time. But I wanted to let him know what I was thinking, including some ideas I'd heard in school.

Obviously, "Fuck that shit, I'm not going!" was a complete misread of the situation because that's when the cannoli started to fly.

My dad's face turned four shades of red as he entered what would later be diagnosed in the Baytown Hospital Emergency Room as an acute hypertensive crisis. My mother, who I could usually count on to be the voice of calm and reason in the family, completely freaked out. "What are you trying to do, kill your father?"

Meanwhile, I just kept ducking the Italian pastry as the conversation rapidly descended into entirely unconstructive ad hominem attacks. Other than a little cannoli in my hair, eyes, and ears, I came out largely unscathed. But it's a memory that still haunts me when I see *any* kind of cream-filled desserts in those refrigerated carousels at the diner.

Who knows if the root cause of the ACC Abortion was the graffiti? With my dad, it could have been anything. Maybe he *never* liked Georgian architecture. He might have decided that College Park was too far to drive after all. Or he just remembered he forgot to fertilize the lawn. Whatever it was, a deathly pall was cast over the car and not a word was spoken until we saw the first signs for the New Jersey Turnpike, 2 hours and 37 minutes later (without traffic).

Finally, I broke the ice. "Well, I guess we can cross Maryland off our list." Everybody had a good laugh at that and then we all played Dump on U. Maryland. My mother thought the campus "wasn't very inviting." My dad asked, "What kind of a name is 'Terrapins' for a football team, anyway?" And he had a point.

I suggested it had been a very productive day. "We ruled out three schools. Two that are too far to drive. And one that isn't but when you get there—there's nothing there!" That brought howls of laughter from both of my parents that filled the car with tears of joy.

"The Great Dreaming Spires of Holder and Cleveland Towers"

With the good times rolling again, I told my parents about my meeting with Miss Brooks, so we decided to take a detour to see the Princeton campus. My mother opened the Rand McNally Large Scale Road Atlas of the Mid-Atlantic States, and it was clear from her immediate reaction that we had just hit geographical desirability pay dirt.

"Exit nine. That wouldn't be a bad drive," she said. "We could take 95 to 78. Or the Belt to the Verrazano," dad replied, relishing the exciting route possibilities the esteemed university could provide us from our home on Long Island. "Either way, it's just a couple hours."

My family was already in love with Princeton just for being where it is on Rand McNally's map. And the love affair only grew once we witnessed "its lazy beauty," as Amory Blaine described it in F. Scott Fitzgerald's big shot debut novel *This Side of Paradise*. I suspect my dad liked the graffiti-free entrance at the FitzRandolph Gate. And *I* was thrilled to get out of the car and stretch my legs after eight hours of driving.

It was one of those ridiculously perfect velvet summer evenings that seemed made for a dusky stroll through the architectural theme park that is the Princeton campus. I breezed past the Romanesque Alexander Hall, the twin white Greek temples of Whig and Clio, and the dour limestone walls of the University Chapel staring down on me like a celibate monk from the Middle Ages. Touring the 600-acre Princeton campus was even better than our visit to Fort Ticonderoga when I was nine, which, until that day, was the gold standard of sightseeing in my family.

About the time I got to the polished stainless-steel panels of George Rickey's kinetic sculpture, *Two Planes Vertical Horizontal II*, I noticed a man in a smart tweed jacket who looked like a professor. He walked on his heels in comfortable shoes with his head tilted to the side as if he was trying to recall some fine distinction between Plato and Socrates that had momentarily slipped his mind.

He led me to Prospect Garden, the scent of impatiens in bloom, until he disappeared into Prospect House, the historic 19th century Italianate mansion where faculty can chill out, chow down, bend an elbow in the tap room and arm wrestle over black holes and the Peloponnesian War.

I imagined that I, too, would be having novel insights about knowledge and morality if I went to school here. "The entire history of human thought walks the halls of these buildings every day," I mused. It was just one of the many profound ideas that started popping into my head like the scarecrow when he received his diploma from the Wizard of Oz.

"Did you see the black squirrels?" my dad asked. "I didn't know Jersey had black squirrels. *Very rare.*" My dad didn't stop talking about the black squirrels all the way home. After we got home. On every holiday visit throughout my four-year undergraduate career. And to the day he died.

The B-Side of Paradise

By the time we got back to Route 1, Princeton was the only name left on my good-fit college list. Though we didn't know it at the time, we had just put all the rational thought into the college selection process that we were going to. My mom liked the different buildings. My dad liked the black squirrels. I liked the professor in the tweed jacket and the sculpture that moved. And nobody wanted to go through another road trip like this one.

So, I boned up on some "two trains" problems, tacked on 180 points to my SATs, Old Jenks wrote me a stellar recommendation, and I was in. Such was the way I went about finding my best-fit college... and Miss Brooks bagged her third Tiger.

If truth be told, there was something about the campus that moved me. It came down to a moment—a feeling I had when I turned to steal one last glance at the stately university on the way back to our new Pontiac Catalina. I remember gazing upon "the great dreaming spires of Holder and Cleveland towers," as Amory Blaine described them, and thinking, amid all the turmoil in the world, "I could be happy here."

Of course, I was seventeen years old, and it had been a very long day. What I did not know at the time, could not have known, was that I was unfit, unbrushed, and unprepared for the Ivy League.

Cells in the Petri Dish of the Great Princeton Lab Experiment

It's hard to express the feelings I had the first day of Orientation Week. Or should I say it's hard to express them in a positive way. What I hadn't anticipated when I first fell in love with the Princeton campus was that I was going to have to share it with 4,000 other people. What it was about Princeton's people that I found less appealing than its Collegiate Gothic architecture is also hard to say.

But it wasn't long after I unpacked the car, waved good-bye to my family, and watched them drive out of sight—about where Elm Street wraps around Dillon Gym's east side—that I had the first of what I would soon refer to as an Uh-Oh, People! moment, when a sense of impending doom would descend on me from nothing more than the sights and sounds of my classmates innocently going about their daily routines.

It sent me into that same gauzy out-of-body region of consciousness I felt when that Princeton football coach and

The B-Side of Paradise

I were watching me from opposite sides of the frosted-glass window of Baytown's hydrotherapy room. I didn't know why this kept happening, but it may have had something to do with F. Scott Fitzgerald. Because on move-in day in the late summer of 1972, when I heard the bell toll on Nassau Hall for the first time, I knew I was in *his* house. And trust me, Old Fitz (the *young* Old Fitz) was *everywhere* that day.

He was dashing through the entryways and sprawled out on the lawns. He was in the sun shining on Blair Arch and in the popped collars on the piqué polos at the Jazz Age lawn party on the hill above the tennis courts. He was the blood in the veins of every great American dreamer who arrived in their family's Town & Country wagon to rejoice in praise of Old Nassau. You see, inside Princeton's ivy-covered walls, like the celluloid heroes in the Ray Davies song, F. Scott Fitzgerald never really dies.

Or maybe I was just feeling a little homesick. After all, I didn't know anybody. And nobody knew me. One would think I would have been prepared for this, but it was the first time since I began my whole godforsaken best-fit-college search that I faced the most disturbing consequence of going away to school. That I wouldn't be taking my high school friends with me. And three of them—Haiku George, Doug, and Charlie, all of whom were confirmed to the belief that "there is *nothing* like a Grateful Dead concert"—would be hard to replace.

My greatest memory of Haiku George was the time he joined me in a prolific display of haiku speedwriting for Mrs. Tancredi's ninth-grade English class. During a fifth period lunch of baked ziti and carrots steamed to within an inch of their lives, we churned out seventy-nine traditional Japanese poems about love and loss, blue fences, hamburger relish, and other traditional poetry prompts, such as the flask of whiskey

Cells in the Petri Dish

Mrs. Tancredi hid in her bottom desk drawer. That was the class's favorite when we read all seventy-nine to them the next day. How do you replace a guy like George?

And Doug, also known as Firesign Doug after he famously mounted the simonized hood of our vice principal's Buick Electra on the first day of Baytown High's Kent State student strike and delivered a rousing tribute to Firesign Theatre's *Waiting for the Electrician or Somebody Like Him*. All 42 minutes of it. From memory.

Even Vice Principal Berry had to admit it was a great performance as he helped him down from the hood, buffing out the scuff marks Doug's Earth Shoes left behind with his Vice Principal shirt sleeve as he did.

Finally, there was Charlie who needs no nickname. By the age of seventeen, Charlie had already lived a lifetime of epic moments. For example, the night he set out between Grateful Dead sets at Roosevelt Stadium to trade a beer for a joint. A rate of exchange he insisted represented parity "once you get past all the hoo-ha about marijuana."

Then it was lights out for Charlie until we found him in the emergency room at the Jersey City Medical Center at three in the morning. All he could remember was driving a hard bargain with some Newark Chapter Hells Angels. Then, "*bam*—red ambulance lights." Almost lost Charlie that night.

What might seem quaint with the distance of time, sent me into something of a panic that day. After failing to find George, Doug, or Charlie—or somebody like them on my search of the lower campus, I returned to my room where in a last-ditch effort to smoke out just one kindred spirit, I sneaked a peek at my roommate Einstein's (because his dad worked with him) record collection. Mahler, Mahler, Mahler. And *State Fair*.

Then I sat down and wrote my first field report from *The B-Side of Paradise*: *Help! I think I've made a terrible mistake. Is it too late to go to Columbia?*

After checking for spelling and punctuation, I slipped the note into an envelope, addressed it to Miss Brooks at Baytown High, and dropped it in the first mailbox I could find. Then returned to my room, hoping she would soon deliver me safely to Morningside Heights, where back in New York, I might have more of a home-field advantage.

Culture-Shock Ray

My second day began with a meet-and-greet for all the first-years in 1915 Hall, hosted by our resident advisor, or R.A., who I will call Ray. One by one we introduced ourselves by name, hometown, and the high school or preparatory school from which we graduated.

Ray told us that Princeton students come from all fifty states, forty-seven countries, and a wide variety of ethnic, racial, religious, and socioeconomic backgrounds. It is not uncommon, he advised, for first-years to have a period of adjustment to the diversity of the student body. A phenomenon he affectionately called culture shock, as if to name it was to tame it.

Ray went so far as to suggest that the culture shock we might feel was something to celebrate. Which was his way of saying "you might think everyone here is a little strange, but so are you, so get over it." But it was too late. I may have been up for a party on day one, but I was no longer in much of a celebratory mood. And no flat-pitched kumbaya from my too-little-too-late resident advisor was going to change that.

Adding insult to injury, when we ran out of cider and donuts (and discomforting tropes from Ray), a cute little first-year in our group approached me and asked if I was related to Mayor Tommy D'Alessandro of Baltimore. When I told her, "No," she said, "Oh." Then turned around and walked away.

Everybody, it seemed, was having difficulty celebrating their culture shock and I was merely one of 1,100 precocious teens dumped into the middle of Central New Jersey searching for their own Haiku George, Doug, or Charlie, trying to stake a claim to their side of paradise before classes began.

Whenever I dumped a rip-your-hair-out story about high school on my father, he always used to tell me—in this tired voice, "Write it down, Al. You have to write it down." You have no idea how I hated the way he said that. But on this day my father's wise counsel was a clarion call. I knew there wasn't a soul in Baytown who would believe a word I had to say about this place without a contemporaneous record. So, I started taking notes...

Pi-Man

Beginning with this slice-of-life drama about Pi-Man, the aerialist/mathlete from Appleton, Wisconsin. I met Pi-Man shuttling between orientation classes and he invited me to his dormitory room. There, he drew my attention to a series of panels of construction paper, each 8½" x 11" in orange, yellow, green, and purple that lined the top perimeter of his walls. A number was neatly stenciled in Times New Roman on each one. When read in sequence, beginning with the familiar 3.14, the numerical series corresponded to the value of the mathematical symbol pi—out to the first 100 decimal places.

But it was more than math-geek wall art. It was also a prop for Pi-Man's theatre of the absurd. "I have it memorized," he said. "Would you like me to recite it?" I was thinking, "No." But he pulled out a bandana and held it over my eyes to demonstrate that there were no transparencies in the fabric. Then he asked me to tie it tightly around his head. Which I did, because, well, what else could I do?

He prompted me to follow along as he recited the full one-hundred-integer sequence without hesitation and without error. Then he ran to his second-story window and jumped out. When I say he jumped out, I mean he hurled his body through the opening in the frame between its sill and head, and its two side-jambs, and disappeared. Fearing that I had just witnessed a classmate leap to his death on just the second day of Orientation Week, all I could think was, "Why me?"

I knew I had to check to see if he was dead or seriously injured from the fall because he might need medical attention. But I hesitated for the briefest moment, wondering whether even the slightest display of concern might advance us down a path of friendship that I was unsure I wanted to take.

Whether from a sense of moral obligation or morbid curiosity, I ran to the window to look down. There I found him dangling in midair, clutching a heavy-gauge manila rope with a wide grin on his face. The rope was attached to a nautical hook he had drilled into the back wall of Hamilton Hall just to facilitate this prank.

"You must have thought I was crazy," he said.

Yeah. I did.

Dudsy's Vast Chain of Disdain

On day three, I met Dudsy (who would later reveal to me that he was a wizard) at a Wilcox Hall mixer. I told him about Pi-Man and asked if he had ever heard the term culture shock. Dudsy, who was from Wyoming, exhibited the clear-minded convictions about things one can only possess growing up in a state with a population density of 5.8 persons per square mile. "Horse spit," he told me. "Culture shock is always their excuse whenever they get caught shopping in the weird mall."

"The thing of it is," he explained, "we are all just cells in the petri dish of the Great Princeton Lab Experiment." Until recent years, Dudsy continued, Princeton just admitted the good ole boys with deep pockets and deep roots into all the usual power structures that have fed into the Ivy League since the seventeenth century.

But now they were taking women and African Americans and lots of public-school losers like himself and me. Of course, they were trying to find the kind of losers who could become winners, he clarified. But it was all new to them and they didn't know what they were doing. Which was why, as he put it, "We are surrounded by a bunch of bodacious circus clowns."

Somewhere between "public school losers" and "bodacious circus clowns," I realized I had met yet another crazy Princeton student. But this one had an eight-pack of Rolling Rock pony bottles and the Spirit album *Twelve Dreams of Dr. Sardonicus*, so, I accompanied him to his room to listen to it along with his conspiracy theories.

"Here's the thing of it," he resolved, "you see, the admissions people hate the students. They think we're just a bunch of entitled brats who don't appreciate the opportunity we've been given." He pressed on, "So, they try to pair up every student with someone who is guaranteed to work their nerves. Then they sit back and laugh at us as we all try to get along." By way of example, Dudsy gave me a rundown of the personality conflicts on his dormitory hall, where everyone was connected in what he called a "vast chain of disdain."

For example: Heidi, from Laurel Canyon, California. Historically a home to movie stars during the Golden Age of Hollywood, Laurel Canyon had become a counter-culture enclave for hit bands of the time, including the Mamas and the Papas, the Byrds, and Buffalo Springfield. To Heidi, everything was at once wholly awesome and a complete mystery, a worldview captured in her favorite expression: "bitchin' whatever?"

Whenever she said "bitchin' whatever?" (which was often), Claire, the cellist from Westchester's Sound Shore, would clear her throat and hum highlights from Bach's *Cello Suite No. 1*, which offended Heidi because Claire wouldn't even acknowledge her presence.

But it really unnerved Jeremy, a wire-haired Physics major with the carefully cultivated look of a young Albert Einstein. Hearing the cello suite (or anything coming out of Claire's mouth from the Baroque period) drove Jeremy nuts. And he would go to his room to blast Steve Reich's *Six Pianos* through his 200-watt-per-channel McIntosh amp.

There he would shovel unhealthy quantities of Cheetos into his mouth to further distance himself from the trappings of eighteenth-century European court society, a practice traced back to him from the orange fingerprints he left on the paper products in the communal bathroom.

The Cheetos dust on the Charmin really pissed-off Ersatz Cowboy Joel because he was both a neat freak and a "live long, die young" longevity fanatic who believed junk food was evil. Dudsy, to complete the vast chain of disdain, thought Ersatz Cowboy Joel was "a horse's ass" and an affront to the proud traditions of the American West.

In fairness, Dudsy offered a pretty good defense of his theory of a corrupt and cynical admissions staff as everyone on his hall, much as he suggested, seemed carefully chosen to annoy one another.

Ersatz Cowboy Joel

The next day I was having dinner in the Wilcox dining room when an honor student and black belt in karate from The Haverford School snapped into a chair across from me and said, "Howdy." He was wearing a Stetson 4X Seneca, silver-sand buffalo felt cowboy hat and a pair of Lucchese western boots, like John Wayne in *True Grit*, a pair of cornflower blue polyester dress slacks (how did he miss the Levi's?), and a pin-stripe short-sleeve button-down shirt in a poly/cotton blend.

I didn't need Columbo to figure out he was Ersatz Cowboy Joel. Other than his mismatched east-meets-western-wear outfit, however, he was relatively normal...if you consider it normal for a teenager to read the *Wall Street Journal* during the college day's most social hour, in the middle of the most social week of an undergraduate's career. Or intermittently break into the chorus of "Brandy (You're a Fine Girl)" from the Jersey Shore band Looking Glass. Often in mid-sentence—his or yours.

Ersatz was a lot to process, for sure, but he didn't invite me to his room to recite the value of pi out to 100 integers and jump out a window. Or grill me on which big city mayor

I was related to. And between choruses of "Brandy," he had a lot of questions for me about Long Island beaches, so, I thought I might like this ersatz cowboy fellow.

There was something intriguing about the way his index-finger carefully coursed up and down the *Journal*'s stock tables as he broke into song. But it was the subtle double-tap of his index finger that preceded every rendition of "Brandy," that was the tell. You see, whenever Ersatz Cowboy Joel invoked Brandy's name, it meant one of his stocks had gone up.

That's when I had my own epiphany about Princeton admissions. "They don't care what kind of music you like," I thought. "If you could be a money-maker, you were in." I can't say that made me feel any better, but I was beginning to reconcile myself to the fact that the Ivy League has its own ideas and I would just have to get used to things as they were.

As history would tell, the Nifty Fifty stock market went off on a wild kegger that year. Ersatz did a lot of singing and, by spring break, he was so flush that he bought a BMW, drove out to California, and never came back. He transferred to UCLA the next year where he received his bachelor's degree, and later a JD and an MBA.

Eschewing the corporate life (or because, who would hire him?), he went out on his own as a bootstrapping, independent venture capitalist specializing in biotech startups and herbal remedy companies. He burned through his inheritance by the time he was twenty-nine. By mid-career, he turned things around and had enough money or credit or secondary inheritance to buy houses in San Diego and Lake Tahoe. Though he never had enough to pay for his dinner whenever he visited me in Manhattan.

Horace Mann's Phone Bill

About the time everybody received their first phone bill, Dudsy knocked on my door holding a thick envelope. "You know, not everybody around here is crazy," he said. "Some people are just having nervous breakdowns." He handed me his phone bill for the line he shared with his roommate, who I will call Horace Mann because that's where he went to high school.

At that time, Jersey Bell itemized long-distance calls on your bill. If you made a lot of calls out of your area, your phone bill could get long. This one was more than 900 long-distance calls long.

"Wow, that's a lot of long-distance calls," I said.

"Do you notice anything about the phone numbers?" Upon closer inspection, I noticed all the calls were to the same phone number.

"Wow, that's a lot of long-distance calls to the same number."

Dudsy prodded me to keep searching deeper into his roommate's pathology. I homed in on each call's duration. There were a lot of 50-minute calls. One lasted a full three hours. And it was common to see one call followed by another—five minutes later. Water break?

Finally, I noticed a pattern of gaps between what Dudsy described as "Horace Mann's coyote cries for help." There were four long ones each day that lasted about 70 minutes: like clockwork, at noon and six p.m., which I figured must have been when he took lunch and dinner.

The other two were consistently at nine a.m. and two p.m. Likely that was while he attended a morning and an afternoon class. Other than that, Horace Mann was on the line with the same number for 327 hours, or every minute of the waking day, over the first month of the semester.

"Ooh," I said. "Your roommate is having a rough time."

"Ya think?"

Horace Mann was an aspiring math genius who in just thirty Ivy League days had hit a wall. He could no longer visualize the mathematical concepts he was learning in class. Dudsy overheard Horace on the phone one day saying, "Mom, I can't visualize it." And then after a brief pause. "*Mom*, you *don't* understand. When you can't see it anymore, IT'S OVER!"

The Primal Scream

There seemed to be no end to the disturbing theatre I was encountering in the Ivy League. One day, when Dudsy pulled out an impressively rolled doober and asked, "Did I ever tell you that I'm a wizard?" I didn't even question him. I just followed.

We walked out to the tennis pavilion on Poe Field where he fired up his perfect cylinder of ground bud. Silently, we passed it back and forth. It was a piney and slightly skunky-scented Ivy League homage to the end of summer. The harvest moon hung low like a lunatic over what we called New New Quad, (because it was even newer than New Quad.)

It's easy not to talk when you're stoned. And we did it, unapologetically, for quite some time, until off in the distance there was a scream: a long primal scream, from an open dormitory window. And there was that feeling again, like I was watching myself watch this guy scream.

"Uh-Oh, People," I said.

"You got that right."

When it ended, what seemed like a lifetime later, the figure in the window pulled his head inside, calmly lowered the window sash, and the room went dark. Like after all that, he decided to just go to bed or take himself out for a snack.

"You know what I think?"

"What, Duds?"

"I think we're adjusting very well to the Ivy League."

I told him I was thinking the same exact thing.

We bought an eight-pack of Rolling Rock pony bottles and spent the rest of the evening toasting one another for our remarkable ability to adapt to our new surroundings… and to the people we had met. We toasted Horace Mann, Ersatz Cowboy Joel, Heidi, Claire, and Pi-Man. We toasted Old Fitz, who in his own Dawn of the Jazz Age way had welcomed us into his house. And we toasted the understanding we had gained about people who were different from us.

Finally, I suggested we toast Carl Jung. Who, I had just read in my psychology textbook, once said, "everything that irritates us about others can lead us to an understanding of ourselves." Dudsy agreed that Jung was toast-worthy.

So, we raised a cold pony to the founder of analytical psychology and called it a night, secure in the knowledge that the more Ivy Leaguers we met, the greater our understanding of ourselves would become.

The Descent

Notes from the
Happy Bottom-Quarter

One of my favorite Princetonians was its seventeenth and surely most amiable president, Bill Bowen. I often saw him walking to Nassau Hall, buttoned up, or as they say in the Ivy League "buttoned down" for a day in the ivory tower: face flushed, hair wet from the Dillon Gymnasium showers after his morning tennis.

Whenever our paths crossed, Bowen would give me a big smile like he was glad to see me. He always made me feel like I belonged. That's all I knew about him, so I thought walking around campus and smiling at me was his job…until my friends told me he was the president of the university. When we discovered he smiled at all of us the same way, we started to refer to him as the university's designated smiler-at-students.

We all agreed he deserved a nickname, and even though there was a bit of Tolkien's good-natured hobbit about him, Bilbo was never meant to be anything more than a shortened form of Bill Bowen. But our Bilbo was more than just a smiling, tennis-playing Bag Ender. He was a labor economist and award-winning author of nineteen books, including *The Game of Life: College Sports and Educational Values* that he co-wrote with James Shulman.

In his 2005 *New Yorker* article "Getting In," Malcolm Gladwell points out an odd confession Bowen makes in the book: He expresses "shame" for the athletic preferences Princeton offered during his tenure only to later reveal results from his own study showing how athletes go on to earn significantly more after college than their Princeton peers. That holds true for what was called at the time "minorities" and students from lower socioeconomic backgrounds.

Gladwell revisits the issue of athletic preferences in his 2014 book, *David and Goliath*, when he traces their origin back to Fred Glimp, Harvard's Director of Admissions in the 1960s. Glimp, as Gladwell tells it, recognized that even elite high school students can wind up at the bottom of the class at Harvard, and for many it can be a painful fall.

What the Cantabs needed, if I may wipe the lipstick off Glimp's pig: some designated losers who could fill the bottom ranks of the class for four years and still go out and be winners in life. These pigs to the academic slaughter would have a special psychological profile due to their achievements outside the classroom that would enable them to feast on a steady diet of Gentleman Bs and even the occasional C-grade slop and still like themselves.

Glimp turned over his cocktail napkin and calculated that he would need to fill a quarter of the class with them to sufficiently pad Harvard's walls so the students whose self-esteem was tied primarily to the classroom wouldn't get hurt when they inevitably go bouncing off. And he called these admits the Happy Bottom-Quarter. Guess where Glimp went looking for "Happy Bottoms?" That's right. On the football field, the soccer and lacrosse fields, the basketball, tennis, and squash courts.

Judging by Bowen and Schulman's study, these Happy Bottoms did just what Glimp thought they would do. They'd rack up a bunch of "very goods" (and the occasional "average") on their report cards, then go out and cash in after graduation. But why would Bilbo Bowen be ashamed of an admissions policy that successfully offered a leg up to the less privileged?

Gladwell says Bowen was engaged in a "skillful deception" when he suggests preferences for athletes (can we just call them jocks?) is an aberration of Ivy ideals. As the Ivy League has long favored the kid who can make the cash register go *ka-ching*. What bothered Bowen, Gladwell writes, was that jocks were "different" from the rest of Princeton's students.

To me, this was a curious case of "othering" in a student body that comes from, to quote my resident advisor Ray's culture-shock lecture from Orientation Week: "all fifty states, forty-seven countries, and a wide range of ethnic, racial, religious, and socioeconomic backgrounds" (all who, in Bowen's telling suddenly, became a utopian mind meld compared to the outlier jocks).

Whatever was bothering Bowen about jocks, it would have been nice if he could have sorted out his feelings before he sent me a thick envelope that memorable spring day oh so many years ago. He could have saved me a lot of trouble.

Happy Bottom-Otherland

So, let's take a walk through Happy Bottom-Otherland on the first day of football practice to see what all the fuss was about. Alas, there was no rest there for this weary B-Sider because the Happy Bottom-Boys at Jadwin Gymnasium were just as intense, ambitious, and bought-in to Old Nassau as every other student. Like their Tiger classmates, they had big appetites for everything on the Ivy League buffet table. And I was still walking around trying to find the dinner plates.

What I hadn't expected was the sophisticated calculations they were already making about how the Friends of Tiger Football who were pacing the sidelines in their straw skimmers and bowties that day might shape their futures. Case in point: Orphan Andy, whom I met while I was working out the combination on my locker.

By way of introduction, Andy cast me a sideways glance and locker whispered, "They say if you make it through four years of Princeton football, the alumni will take care of you," like he was cutting me in on the latest shipment of crack cocaine from Miami. Andy was just one of a type of first-gen kids I met in the locker room who were living with the fevered dream that some great white Tiger alum would finger them for the Daddy Warbucks treatment.

Then there were the country club boys who were strapping on their pads and measuring the drapes for their corner offices at the same time. They were already on a first-name basis with Princeton's tailgating elite. "Hey, Pinky. Looking good." "Atta boy, Penny." These were the "big swinging dick" Wall Street alpha males that Michael Lewis described in his book *Liar's Poker*. In fact, more than one of my teammates in the locker room that day wound up on Michael Milken's junk bond team at Drexel Burnham Lambert—and in Lewis's book.

As for me, I knew I was a little too independent to expect a benediction from any of the Jazz Age skeletons eager to meet the new Tiger litter that day. I was just hoping I could find a Haiku George, Doug, or Charlie in pads somewhere in that locker room.

Back at Baytown High, if you wanted to make friends, it never hurt to take a sarcastic jab at the nearest authority figure or stuffy old institution. So, I seized on my opportunity when the equipment manager handed out 100 pairs of not so gently used (and technologically obsolete) square-toed high-top football cleats. They looked like Amory Blaine himself might have worn them when he wrenched his knee in practice and was forced to retire to life in the Triangle Club and the *Daily Princetonian.*

"Are they kidding with these high-tops?"

Words I hoped would elicit a round of empathetic responses from a soulmate or two, instead bounced off every hard surface in the room until there was not a single Happy Bottom spared from my offense. Rather than a "tell me about it" or a high five, my words set off a gentle roll of raised eyebrows that moved through the room like a silent stadium wave and turned every Happy Bottom face to stone.

Message sent: There would be no criticizing Princeton equipment or Princeton anything else in this locker room.

"China Cat Sunflower"

The first week the football team had split practice sessions. The offense practiced at three with the offensive coordinator and the defense followed at four-thirty with the defensive coordinator. Cocky SOB that I was, I spent most of the first two days sizing up who I thought would quit before the week was out, and who I thought wouldn't but should.

On the third day, I ran into Coach Robertson, the

phantom behind the frosted-glass window in Baytown's hydrotherapy room. He was happy to see that I had chosen to join his squad. "Hey, I see you decided to come out for defense," he said. "That's fantastic. Good to have you on board." Of course, I hadn't decided anything of the sort. I was at the wrong practice.

Unprepared for this kind of setback so early in my career, and more than a little embarrassed, I ran through my options. I could tell the phantom I had made a mistake, bid a hasty retreat to my dorm, and try to get to the correct practice the next day. This was my worst option because I would get docked for missing a practice *and* for being stupid.

Or I could practice with the defense, just to be polite, and return to the offensive team's practice the next day with a sheepish mea culpa. This was a better bet, as I would get credit for showing commitment to the team, though questions would persist about my ability to follow a simple schedule.

Or I could switch teams as if that had been my intention all along. This option had obvious benefits, as I would be blameless in any capacity. Except that I would be stuck with the decision for the next four years. And I wasn't sure I wanted to play defense.

It was an issue I wasn't happy to have to sort out on the spot, especially with the flint-eyed apparition Robertson still smiling at me. I could tell this was shaping up to be one of those "should I stay or should I go?" moments. One had to ask themselves: "What is it that I truly want?" And all I wanted to do was go home, shut my door to the world, and listen to "China Cat Sunflower." So, that's exactly what I did.

Once Coach Robertson was out of sight, I bolted the athletic center like Michael Corleone skipping the bill at Louie's Restaurant. "Just let your hand drop to your side and the gun slip out.... walk out of the place real fast.... Don't look nobody directly in the eye..." All that was missing was Sollozzo and McCluskey lying dead on the floor, and Tessio waiting outside in a '54 Packard to take me back to the family compound in Emerson Hill.

And, of course, instead of going into exile in Sicily, I went back to my dorm room, dropped side two of *Europe 72* down the spindle of my trusty (if somewhat pedestrian by Ivy League standards) Garrard Zero 100 turntable, reached for my tennis racket, and air-guitared "China Cat Sunflower" into "I Know You Rider" three times. This time-honored Dead Head practice sustained me for the better part of two weeks.

Fritz Crisler's Winged Helmet

Until I received a phone call from the varsity football coach, who I will call Tiger McLore (for reasons you will soon understand). Always a sucker for a good line, he had me with, "What's the matter, you don't like this part of campus?" So, when he invited me to his office, thinking there might be food involved, I accepted.

I found him at his desk surrounded by a meticulously curated exhibit of Princeton football memorabilia that looked like it might have been staged for our meeting. There was an F. Earl Christy hand-painted mug from 1905 on his desk and a framed program from a 1956 Penn game on his wall, but it was Coach McLore's comprehensive history of Princeton football that really set the tone for our meeting.

Princeton's gridiron saga was as long as the story of football itself. In fact, the first American football game ever (EVER) was played in 1869 by Rutgers and the College of

The B-Side of Paradise

New Jersey (which was Princeton's name before it decided to downplay its association with the Garden State). Princeton also had its paws all over the first college football rules ever written. They helped pen them in 1876 with some rule-writing types from Columbia, Harvard, and Yale.

And (sit down for this one), with fifteen NCAA recognized national championships under its belt, Princeton was tied with the University of Alabama for the second-most in college football history. I did *not* see that one coming.

McLore's knowledge of Princeton football's 103-year history was exhaustive. Some of the highlights he shared with me that day included Coach Herbert "Fritz" Crisler's development of the winged helmet in 1935, and a colorful profile of Dick Kazmaier, Princeton's only Heisman Trophy winner.

In the interest of reciprocity, I thumbed my brain to recollect my own history, in case Coach should say, "Well that's ours. Tell me yours." I was prepared to go back to D'Alessandro Field, where my career began on a half-acre plot bordering the Pell Estate, lined with Norway spruces, two white firs for accent, and a hedge of forsythias that yielded yellow flowers in the spring.

It was a grand arena for such humble beginnings where the action amounted to little more than me emulating the stumbles and tumbles I saw on TV football—in slow motion, where football was little more than an elaborate game of "all fall down." Think: "London Bridges" in shoulder pads.

One day I cut my friend Bugs in on the finer points of slow-motion football, and we formed the Bugs D'Alessandro Football League, or the BDFL, complete with eight teams, league standings, and stats we would register in a marble notebook after each game. Slow-motion football was more of a pas de deux than an arena sport. It prioritized aesthetics over traditional football's territorial imperative to advance a ball over a goal line. It rested on three principles.

1. Respect the speed limits. Speed up to elude a tackle (or make one) and you draw a flag.

2. Obey the torque. If you initiate a football move resulting in contact that (by the laws of physics) would naturally result in a fall, you must go down and do so in a realistic and aesthetically pleasing manner that simulated the pro moves seen on TV.

3. The Equal Protection Clause: Everyone must have an equitable chance to fall and make the other guy fall, or Bugs would start crying and go home.

McLore wrapped up our colloquy on Tiger Football with the suggestion that I return to the field for the honor of being part of Princeton's great gridiron tradition. I tried to explain that I could care less about Princeton football tradition. I was in as long as it was fun like the BDFL was for Bugs and me. The history of which I was able to touch on only briefly as he clearly had no intention of listening to my stories the way I had so patiently listened to his.

He abruptly asked me when I was going to return to practice: "Today or tomorrow?" I chose tomorrow after briefly considering a request for forty-eight hours because I had tickets for that night's Dead show at the Spectrum and anticipated being wasted the next day. Then I thought that might be pushing it. Twenty-four hours later, still a little ripped from the night before, I dutifully laced up Amory Blaine's square-toed high-tops and returned to the field.

"Stay Down Luke"

As one might expect, I received less than a cordial reception from the other Happy Bottoms who had dutifully remained chained to the medieval torture chamber that is pre-season football practice the past ten days, while I was playing lead guitar for a popular psychedelic rock-and-roll band in my head. Trust me, nobody likes it when you skip your turn on the old thumbscrew.

Week after week, the coaches pinned the depth chart to the locker-room wall and there I was at the bottom. One day, opportunity knocked. I had the good fortune to do some things in practice I was sure would boost me up the charts to my rightful position on top. Yet, at the end of the week, I remained (conspicuously, in my view), on the fifth string. That's when I decided it was time for a little self-advocacy and I went to chat with the first-year coach, Arnie Willson.

Coach Arnie gave me what can only be described as a confused look. "I just figured you were staying out this year to get invited to varsity camp next year," he said as if it was something decreed from above. Which I suspect it was. And that explained why I seemed to be invisible to the guys making out the depth chart.

I had a different idea. Seeing that I had extended Coach McLore's stories far more courtesy than he did mine (and, frankly, more than I really cared to at the time), I felt a little giveback was in order. So, because I had a bit of a mouth in those days, I suggested, "How 'bout I come out next year for next year. And I play this year for this year?"

That afternoon, on the eve of our game with the University of Pennsylvania, Coach Arnie rounded up the team to watch the tight ends face off with the defensive linemen in the much-dreaded drill called the Nutcracker. It's a medieval joust kind of affair where two players run and crash into each other until someone falls to the ground.

Although I didn't know it at the time, it was a pre-arranged "depth chart duel" that Coach Arnie cooked up to give me a chance to dig myself out of the hole I was in. There were five tight ends and ten defensive linemen, so, naturally we got worn down first. After several rotations, the other tight ends began to drop out until I was the last man standing.

I got down in my three-point stance, shot out when I heard "go," and banged into some relative stranger until one of us fell to the ground. Then I got back up and did it again and again and again until even the defensive linemen began to drop out. It was like that scene in *Cool Hand Luke* where Paul Newman keeps getting up to fight George Kennedy except nobody was saying "Stay down, Luke."

One Nutcracker blended into another, until it was all an exercise in muscle memory. That's when Coach Arnie caught me off guard. He got right up in my face and demanded an answer to a question I hadn't seen coming: "Who just drove my best defensive end downfield ten yards and put him on his butt?" And I was, like, "Really? You're giving me a test, now?"

At least, that's what I would have liked to say. But all I could muster was, "I don't know, Coach. I don't know." They immediately put me through concussion protocol, such as it was at the time. Then told me to go inside and clean myself up. That's when I noticed there was a crime scene on my formerly white jersey that was now completely soaked in blood from, as these things tend to go in football, my nose that was very broken.

On my way out of the field house, toilet tissue dams in both nostrils, I ran into my only confidante on the team. I will call Pablo (because he was a fine arts student and an abstract painter). He asked me if I had seen the new depth chart and gave me a big pat on the back for some reason. I just said, "Yes." I don't know why I said yes. I guess I was a little woozy.

The Three Sophomores Across the Hall

After dinner, I heard hooting, yowling, and other feral sounds coming from the Three Sophomores Across the Hall's room. One of them, who I will call Clogs (because he wore them), invited me to their Med School Dreams Go Up in Smoke Party.

The festivities were in celebration of their Organic Chemistry exam, that they referred to as "laughably hard" and likely signifying the end of their medical careers. Someone dropped the needle on the new Yes album, *Close to the Edge*, and because I could always rally for Yes, I said, "Okay, just for a bit. I have a game in the morning."

When Steve Howe hit the first acoustic chords on "And You And I," the hash pipe came out. After each of them had had a healthy draw, Clogs passed me the pipe. "No, thanks. I have a game in the morning." And for some reason, everyone thought that was funny.

Anyway, the last thing I remember was saying, "Okay, maybe just one hit." Before I woke up at ten twenty-three the next day for our ten o'clock game in Philadelphia. Prayers that hadn't passed my lips since my Confirmation were streaming through my head like a news bulletin. I quickly ran through my options.

And there weren't any. There was no way I could get to Franklin Field in Philadelphia from 1915 Hall on the Princeton campus in negative 23 minutes. So, I crawled back into bed where I couldn't help but wonder if all this might be happening because I turned my back on Christ in the tenth grade.

I woke again at noon. On the way to the shower, I passed the mirror over my dresser. At first, I thought it would be best to avoid looking straight into it but couldn't resist a glance. And there I was. Smiling. Just as Fred Glimp predicted, there are some people who have an unshakeable fondness for themselves, no matter how badly they mess things up. And in that kingdom, I wore the crown.

I would have liked to find a more graceful exit to my gridiron career. I think things could have been very different if I had just kept my mouth shut about those square-toed high-tops. But I couldn't. I never can.

Basking in the Unconditional Love of Bilbo Bowen

It would have been reasonable for me to ask myself: What's next? What does a bottomed-out Happy Bottom, who prides himself on accomplishments outside the classroom, do when he no longer has accomplishments outside the classroom? For the time being, I decided it would be best to kick back to see what the world decides to do with me.

I watched, with more than casual interest, as the cosmos, in its infinite wisdom, lured me to PJ's Pancake House for some "old west" buckwheat pancakes. On the way, I ran into Pablo, my football confidante, as he was making his way back to his dormitory room in Holder Hall after the game.

"*Dude,* where *were* you?"

"Oh, that," I said.

"*Dude,* Arnie packed your bag and brought it on the bus."

"Really?"

"He held the driver up to wait for you."

"Really?"

"You were going to start, man. Didn't you see the depth chart?"

"Yeah, I might have missed that."

This was going to be a tough one to explain at Thanksgiving. I envisioned festive autumnal pies winging past my ears sometime between the Macy's Thanksgiving Day Parade and the Detroit Lions game. I knew the disc-shaped harvest-time desserts would require different ducking maneuvers than the ones I employed for the Flying Christmas Cannoli. And I wondered if the seasonal spices would sting when I was cleaning pumpkin filling out of my eyes and ears, days—if not weeks—later.

When I got to Cannon Green, I saw a familiar face. It was Bilbo Bowen, the award-winning author, economist, and designated-smiler-at-students. He turned to me in passing with his usual broad-faced greeting. For a warm and peaceful moment, I stood there, basking in the unconditional love of Bilbo Bowen. In pads or out, he made me feel like I would always be valued at Princeton.

At least that's how I felt at the time. Now, seeing how he threw me under the bus in his book, I guess I really didn't know what President Bowen was thinking after all.

The Case of the
Purloined Grocery Cart

When the Princeton admissions office sent my letter of acceptance roughly a half century ago, they never could have imagined it would lead to the brink of an international crisis. Or that I would become the prime suspect in a kidnapping attempt—an alleged kidnapping attempt—of a classmate. Specifically, a matter involving a member of an important family from a country of interest to American intelligence.

Of course, I was completely innocent. Sort of. More importantly it was my faithful testimony that defused the situation. What's worth revisiting, however, for those who marvel at the way history unfolds, is just how easy it was to make the hairs on the backs of the heads of the powers that be stand straight up. At least it was for me. Not to brag, but everybody must be good at something.

All I needed to turn an ordinary Ivy League evening into a night of diplomatic intrigue was a member of a royal family from a nation whose government was propped up by the CIA; what we used to call a fifth, but now call a 750 ml bottle of Southern Comfort; a road-tripping friend from high school named Trouble; a prank caller; and an ordinary grocery cart. Plus, the element of chance. Namely, the improbable event that student housing would assign a room to a Middle Eastern prince directly above mine.

To protect his identity, I will give him the name Tony Safavieh. Prince Tony, as I knew him, which was not at all, appeared to be mild mannered, handsome, and well-groomed. A casual but neat dresser with a preference for American blue jeans and short sleeve chambray shirts.

He was not the type you would expect to find shot-gunning beers at a toga party, tossing his lunch in a beer-pong tournament, or with his head out the window of 1915 Hall screaming *"Fuck meeeee!"* in the middle of midterms.

This is not to suggest he was some sort of ceremonious snob. He was just a laid-back guy trying to find himself and get an education without stirring up a lot of dust—much like the rest of us. He was the kind of person who gives monarchies a good name. It saddens me to think that I caused him any trouble.

Speaking of Trouble, he caught me by surprise when he knocked on my door that night. "I'm surprised that you're surprised because I sent you a letter to expect me."

"Your *letter* surprised me."

Did you read it?"

"I did."

"Then why are you surprised?"

"I remember reading it and thinking, I'll be surprised if he actually shows up.'"

"Ah, so that explains it."

The important thing is, Trouble came to my door, I was there, and I was happy to see him. I liked Trouble—the person, not the state or condition. And it's always good to see an old friend, especially when you're experiencing a rocky adjustment to your first year in college.

Obviously, Trouble is not his real name. But I call him Trouble, well, because he was. And he had a predilection for getting us involved in nettlesome entanglements going back to sophomore year in high school. He was always trying to get me to do things like hop people's fences, jump in their pools and run away before the police arrived.

Trouble came from a prominent family in our town and had a sense of entitlement, the likes of which I could only have dreamed. And he was always tempting fate. Like the time he lit a doober driving on Upper Baytown Road and passed it to me under the advisement, "Be discreet, there's a cop behind us."

Now the average person, especially in the days when they still sent suburban youths to jail for possession, might consider a squad car in their rearview mirror a prompt *not* to light a joint. But Trouble was not the average person.

That said, when he wasn't baiting local law enforcement, he routinely conformed to the social conventions of the day. This is how the variable of the bottle of Southern Comfort entered the equation. Because Trouble knew that a guest never shows up empty-handed.

"Princeton students are weird," he announced when we got over our initial surprise. "No, I mean *really*, weird. I met some on my way and they're not anything like Colgate students." Then he handed me the bottle of Southern Comfort. "I think we'll be needing this."

I thought this validation from someone I knew from home might do me some good, because there was nobody that could help you take your mind off your (*sorry*) troubles like Trouble. "Some of them don't even look at you when you speak to them."

"It's an interesting cast of characters we have here," I said.

"If by 'interesting,' you mean terrifying." He went on to explain that they had weird people at Colgate, too, but they were polite enough to skulk around campus alone and usually in the shadows. "Here, they travel in packs. It's like they feel empowered."

Over the next hour, we toasted high school memories, like the time our Physics teacher managed to cram "be that as it may," "such as it is," and "ipso facto" all in the same sentence—a syntactical feat whose degree of difficulty is off the charts, and one that we both agreed had to defy at least one of the laws of Physics he had taught us. Though neither of us could say which one.

And we toasted Trouble's surviving an encounter, on his way from the bus stop on Nassau Street to 1915 Hall, with what he insisted, "surely must be the worst kind of Princeton students behaving badly." Namely, the university's famed acapella group the Nassoons singing "Perfidia" unapologetically in Blair Arch. A performance he characterized as "a jarring anachronism."

Considering it was that same day in history that Curtis Mayfield's *Superfly* album reached number one on the Billboard 200, he had a point. So, we toasted "Superfly," even though we couldn't remember much of the words beyond, "Oh, Superfly... something, something, something." And "Ah-ha-ha," which we sang in our best 20-feet-from-stardom voices.

You never forget your first college visit from a friend from back home. Or what you were drinking. And this story can't be told without additional background on our compatibility as drinking buddies. Because there was none. Without question, the night would have unfolded very differently if he had chosen something from our otherwise well-worn path to the refrigerated section of the liquor store; something with an ABV of, say, five percent.

You see Trouble was one of those drinkers who can be described as having a hollow leg. I, on the other hand, could get very happy on two beers. At four, throbbing pains would emerge over my left temple, often accompanied by extreme sensitivity to sound and light. Anything after that was just an exercise in masochism. The good news was that my alcohol intolerance prevented me from binge drinking…on most occasions.

The exception of course, was when spirits were on the beverage program. Anything 80 proof, if pounded hard and fast, could get me "too happy" before the pain kicked in—my signal to stop. That's why Trouble's host gift of the fifth of Southern Comfort was critical to the way events proceeded. That night we drank particularly hard, and fast. And we went from hello to *woot–woot* in record time. Then the phone rang.

"Hello." "Hello? "Hello!" Enter the prank caller. I'm not talking about the kind who asks "Do you have Prince Albert in a can? Well, let him out." This was one of those silent prank callers. The worst kind. Wordlessly, this person would lead me to what was, figuratively speaking, the door of the palace and literally the scene of the (alleged) crime.

"Weird," Trouble said as I hung up the phone. Then it rang again. And again. And again. Ring. "Hello." Silence. Ring. "Hello." Silence. Ring. "Hello. Who is this? Why are you calling me? You don't understand we have a bottle of Southern Comfort here."

There was the occasional lull that allowed us to resume

our celebration of toast-worthy people and events in our lives before the prank would begin again. Had we been drinking our customary American-style lager, I'd like to think I would have had the presence of mind to simply *rip the fucking cord out of the wall.* Such a remedy would have, but for that smooth drinking whiskey they call The Spirit of New Orleans, saved us all a lot of, well you know...

Worse still, I convinced myself that I knew precisely who the caller was. Namely, one of the three sophomores across the hall: Dr. Jolly, the mischievous pre-med Romanian from Brazil.

It was a simple process of elimination. After just six weeks on campus, I had no enemies and few friends...at least none that I could identify outside of the sophomores across the hall and Dudsy—the wizard who told me about the Great Princeton Lab Experiment. That some people would call a conspiracy theory, but he called "just the facts"; the same tight-joint-rolling Dudsy who introduced me to *The Twelve Dreams of Dr. Sardonicus,* the seminal album by the one-hit wonder band Spirit. Not exactly the description of a prank caller.

I also quickly ruled out the other two sophomores across the hall. Clogs, I knew for a fact, was home in Philadelphia for the weekend. And the third sophomore across the hall, who Clogs and Dr. Jolly often referred to as Hyper was just not the prank caller type. It had to be Jolly.

As Trouble and I steadily advanced in our race to the bottom of the fifth of Southern Comfort, I cleverly decided to call Jolly—the prankster—myself, just to let him know I was on to his game. But Jolly, ever the tactician, didn't answer.

Moments later, the phone rang again.

This time, I put Trouble on the line and snuck across the hall to Jolly's door. There were no signs of life inside. No sounds. No light spilling through the door sill or jambs. But that didn't fool me. Jolly was just the kind of guy to prank call in the dark. Something only an advanced crank could do, considering all the dormitory phones had unlit rotary dials.

However, I knew it was possible to dial a rotary phone in a pitch-black room. Having done it myself, flat on my back with a pillow over my head dialing for weed at one in the morning.

All one must do is find the first hole on the finger wheel with your index finger and count as you carefully inchworm from one finger hole to the next until you reach the destination: the first digit in the phone number. Then slowly spin the dial clockwise until you reach the finger stop. Retrace your path, never removing your finger from the hole, until you return to your starting point. Then repeat the process six more times until you have dialed the full number.

With all the evidence pointing to Jolly, I knocked on his door. "Jolly, I know you're in there." But there was no response. There didn't seem to be much point in remaining in the hall where I was barefoot and there was a cold breeze whistling in from an early autumn frost. So, I returned to my room where Trouble was waiting for me.

"I invited the caller over for a drink, but they hung up," he reported. "Whoever it is, they're not very friendly. I don't think they even like Southern Comfort." And then the phone rang.

"Aha," I said. "He hung up when he heard me in the hall. Then called again as soon as I returned." I saw this as clear evidence he had to be in the dormitory because he knew my comings and goings. "Or maybe they live in a different dorm but just had to take a bathroom break," Trouble suggested.

It was just the kind of flat-world thinking one might expect from a Colgate student. But nothing could throw me off Jolly's scent now. If he was not in his room, where could he be? And that's how the prank caller connected me to the scene of the crime.

Knowing he was friendly with Prince Tony's roommate, I decided he must be in the Royal Suite. So, I ran upstairs to the palace door, one of two dormitory rooms on a hallway about the size of a landing in a converted Manhattan brownstone.

"Don't you think we've had enough fun for one night, Jolly?"

A line that, had it been in a Hollywood movie, would be a shoo-in for the American Film Institute's *100 Years…100 Movie Quotes*. I suspect it would have landed somewhere between "Here's looking at you, kid," and "Go ahead, make my day." To think that I improvised it in the state that I was in… So much talent wasted all these years.

I don't know why I expected Jolly to rush out and confess to the crime like a fevered perp in a Perry Mason episode, but for some reason I was caught off guard when the door didn't open. It was then I realized that my hands were wrapped around the handle of a grocery cart. More to the point, with 375 milliliters of Southern Comfort in me, one might say that *I* was wrapped around the handle of a grocery cart.

Before I explain how it came to be that the front of that shopping cart *came into contact* (crashing is too strong a word) with Prince Tony's door, it is worth considering how unlikely it was for it to be there in the first place.

Grocery carts on above-ground dormitory halls may be prevalent at other colleges where they have high-rise dorms with elevators. But most of the student housing at Princeton was in low-rise walk-ups. The chances of finding a grocery cart on the second floor of a walkup residence hall were smaller than the possibility of interacting with royalty. You can take my word on this, as there is only one story in this book about a grocery cart while there are two about members of royal families.

In fact, grocery carts were rarely seen in any campus quarters because the need to transport more food supplies than one can carry out of a market by hand is very low. Most students have meal plans and the only dormitory suites with kitchenettes were in Spelman Hall. And I have it on good authority those kitchens were only used for cleaning bongs. What's more, the percentage of students who had a refrigerator larger than a mini was small.

Of course, Prince Tony could have been one of those rare students with a full-size refrigerator. Assuming he was, it is possible that he and his roommate decided to stock up on beer, soda, and Dannon yogurt that day. Having bought more than they could transport by hand, they were left with no choice but to commandeer the cart; surely, they fully intended to return it.

But that would only explain why the prince and his roommate might have purloined it in the first place. It doesn't explain why they brought it up to the second floor, because if the groceries were too unwieldy to lug up the stairs in one trip, they would only be prohibitively more so if they brought the cart along with them.

I am not sure if all global strife is as enigmatically born as the Case of the Purloined Grocery Cart, but something like fate put my hands on that cart's handle. And when Jolly didn't answer, well, you can't fight fate, as they say.

The reader may be visualizing some loud and violent Hollywood scene: the cart crashing, the door splintering, hinges swaying. But the most dramatic thing that happened on the other end of the grocery cart was a dull thud. The doors in 1915 Hall were indestructible, made of 2-inch thick, reinforced hardwood. The gates to the Safavieh Palace were virtually unblemished.

They did have very sensitive deadbolts, however, that would jam with so much as the *kiss* of a grocery cart. Even the more fiendish attack my own door suffered at the hands of an enraged neighbor wielding an eighty-pound barbell (details to come in the next chapter) did little more.

All the same, when Prince Tony returned to his room that evening, he couldn't open his door. So, he went to the Proctor's office. The Princeton Office of the Proctor, according to a 2014 article in the *Princeton Alumni Weekly*, was established in 1870, by then university President James McCosh, and its staff memorialized in a spirited student song from the 1930s as the "Pinkertons of Princeton."

The idea that the university employed a team of private detectives watching your every move (or at least mine, after that night) always seemed a little creepy to me. It wasn't so much that they went looking for trouble as they were looking to keep the students out of trouble. Or, more specifically, to keep the town police out of student affairs. You never can tell whose parents are running the state department or the state of New Jersey.

Most students who were not involved in the illicit drug trade or hardened criminals of one kind or another looked upon the university proctors as a benevolent group. However, faced with a felony offense like abduction, they could come off as forbidding figures. And that's exactly how they looked to me when they entered our room that night and where they, incidentally, found me and Trouble—and Jolly.

"Some weird guy came by looking for you, so I offered him a drink," Trouble advised when I discovered him partying with Jolly. "And, by the way, I don't think he's the prank caller." With that, Jolly handed me his Amtrak ticket as evidence that he was traveling from Philadelphia, where he was visiting Clogs, during the time in question. With his punched stub in hand, I made a mental note to strike detective work from my list of possible careers.

The proctors, on the other hand, didn't appear to be in much of a partying mood. Which is not to say they weren't chatty. In fact, they had a lot of questions to ask us, such as: How long had we been in our room? Did we notice any disturbances? Had we seen any strangers or heard any loud noises? Can we recount with detail our whereabouts between eight-fifteen and nine forty-five that evening?

It didn't take much to convince them that we had been chained to a bottle of Southern Comfort for the entirety of the evening. But their probing questions made us curious. So, we decided to ask them one. "Why do you ask?"

And then the good Proctor Clarence told us they were investigating an attempted kidnapping. "A kidnapping?" I asked. "Who would want to kidnap anyone here?" Then Jolly, who apparently was more cut out for detective work than me, suggested, "Tony. They kidnap people like him in his country. It's in the newspapers all the time."

"Whoa..." I said, in that stupid all-purpose drunken/stoned-out refrain we used at the time to express amazement with almost any declarative statement. It didn't really come together for me, though, until Proctor Clarence elaborated. "We believe there was an attempted breach on his door. They didn't get in, but the lock is jammed."

It was instructive to see how fast one can sober up when called upon to mount a defense against a Class B felony charge punishable by fifteen to thirty years in a New Jersey state prison. In less time than it took for that grocery cart to jam Prince Tony's deadbolt, my mind cleared. My speech was no longer slurred. My mental judgement advanced the equivalent of five maturational years to the age where emerging science about brain development says the young male brain finally reaches full maturity.

Understanding the gravity of the situation, I came clean. "That was me," I said as if it was a surprise to myself. "I mean, I wasn't trying to kidnap anybody…but that was me."

Recognizing this was no time to play charades, I told them everything. About my road tripping friend, Trouble. The fifth of Southern Comfort. The prank caller. How I pleaded with the caller to stop. How I came to believe Dr. Jolly was the caller. And I went to confront him at his door. Absent there, I told the good proctors that I suspected he was in the prince's room and went looking for him on the second floor.

I explained that that was where, against all odds, I discovered the purloined grocery cart. Next, I told them how I stopped to reflect on how improbable it was that the cart came to be there, because I thought it was important for them to ponder the randomness of life much as I had on the landing to Prince Tony's room that evening. And finally, I described how the cart *encountered* the door, again deciding that *crashing* would be too strong a word.

They were very relieved and even grateful, due, I suspect, to the useful detail if not the philosophical perspective I provided their investigation. And, I think, because honesty is highly valued amongst people in their line of work. Finally, we offered them the last swig of Southern Comfort, but they had to refuse because they were on duty. Which we expected, but we were brought up to always offer.

That was pretty much the end of the Case of the Purloined Grocery Cart, except that I had to pay $60 to fix the door. Then Trouble, Jolly, and I went out to the Colonial Restaurant for pizza and beer. We talked about how strange it had all been to be under investigation like that. I extended my apologies to Prince Tony through Jolly, who was a pretty good friend of his. He said he would pass it on and that we shouldn't sweat it, "Tony will be cool with it."

All of which brings us back to Fred Glimp and his Happy Bottom-quarter-admissions policy. Fred, I suspect, never thought his groundbreaking theory would ever lead to anything like the Case of the Purloined Grocery Cart. To refresh your memory, Happy Bottoms like me were supposed to take the pressure off the other students, not kidnap them. This speaks to the old saw that the law of unintended consequences is the only one that works all the time.

Had the evening turned out differently for the good Prince Tony Safavieh, then the title of this story might have been something like "The Night Fred Glimp's Bed Fell (with all due respect to James Thurber), because any Happy Bottom threat to the crown would have brought his admissions policy tumbling down. In such case, you might have read my name in a Malcolm Gladwell book instead of his name in mine. And I might have gone down in history as the Typhoid Mary of Ivy League Football.

Only time will tell on the other hand, if I will be remembered as the Happy Bottom who saved Ivy League athletic preferences. Fortunately for those who enjoy fall tailgating parties in Hanover, New Hampshire, to the north; and Philadelphia to the south; Ithaca to the west and Cambridge to the east, Ivy League athletic preferences have survived to this day. Depending on how you feel about that, you may take a moment now to cheer or jeer.

The Abbreviated
Wrestling Match

Compared to most colleges, student housing at Princeton was lavish. My son Beckett, for example, lived with two roommates in a 180-square-foot cinderblock cell his first year at one of those trendy and outlandishly expensive colleges on the outskirts of Boston, while I shared 800 square feet of solid oak floors and crown molding spread out over three rooms with mine.

Despite the stately digs, it was common to hear classmates' despair, "I wish I had a single." Private accommodations were hard to come by for first-years but not impossible. All you had to do was demonstrate that your housing situation was a danger to your mental health and/or physical well-being. I met both requirements (resoundingly) after the Abbreviated Wresting Match.

Of course, there are pros and cons to flying solo. On the positive side, it meant I didn't have to worry about getting hit over the head with a set of barbells by one of the three sophomores across the hall. On a less sanguine note, I had to wake to the sounds of Roberta Flack singing "Killing Me Softly" on my music alarm clock every morning, with no one around to talk me down off the ledge. One day, the song beat me into a shapeless mass of insecurity and self-doubt, and I began to question life itself.

The Ethnic Slur Heard Round the World

The earliest roots of the night of the Abbreviated Wrestling Match—the night I earned my single room the hard way— can be traced to an ethnic slur launched like a mortar shot by one of the three sophomores across the hall, Clogs. I had just stepped out of 1915 Hall when he spotted me from the hill above the tennis courts, a good sixty yards away, and called out, "Hey, how'd your dago?"

I first understood this greeting as, "How'd your day go?" But quickly was able to unwrap its double-entendre, thanks to my favorite read at the age of seven, *The Yogi Berra Story*. It was there, in Gene Roswell's incisive biography of the man who once said, "We're lost. But we're making good time," that I learned the term "dago." The term was, as Roswell told it, commonly used to refer to Italians who lived in the south St. Louis neighborhood known as Dago Hill.

Had I not been such a voracious reader at seven, the epithet might have gone over my head. Seeing that "wop" and "greaseball" were the coin of the realm in my old Baytown stomping grounds. By the time I realized that The Haverford School boys took their linguistic cues from the high school dropouts from St. Louis' Little Italy circa 1942, Clogs was gone.

The B-Side of Paradise

This was all back in the days when ethnic slurs were still popular on Ivy League campuses so, I was less thrown by Clogs' affront than by its manner of delivery. In Baytown, when someone wanted to insult your heritage, they did it up close and personal; not from infantry support range.

And they usually had a pack of Marlboro cigarettes rolled up in the sleeve of their T-shirt and a mirror shine on their Cuban-heeled boots when they did, rather than the classic blue Swedish clogs favored by my Main Line Philadelphia friend from across the hall.

Having grown up amongst Brooklyn émigrés, I knew how the game was played, and I knew Clogs expected a response in kind to his flatline groaner. So, the next time he hit me with, "Hey, how'd your dago?" I responded with the equally recumbent, "Fine, how 'bout Jew?"

Despite our repartee having about as much bounce as a dead cat, Clogs seemed to like it and this became our official greeting for, well, forever. He never got tired of it. Such was the price I had to pay for camaraderie in my still early days on *The B-Side of Paradise*.

Naturally these breaches of etiquette brought us closer together. And I soon became the adopted roommate of the three sophomores across the hall. That's how I met Dr. Jolly, the mischievous pre-med Romanian from Brazil. Who was *not* the crank caller in the Case of the Purloined Grocery Cart—or so he claims.

Jolly was one of those polite foreign students who could never understand why Americans were always insulting each other. "Why do you say these things?" he would ask. We used to tell him it was complicated. (Because it was.) And he would say, "It's very strange."

Then he would throw his hands over his head and follow

up with, "What the hell, let's go to Colonial for a pizza." I believed this to be his idea of a gesture of assimilation, reflecting his understanding that all disputes in America are resolved, allowing for geographic variations, by going to Colonial for a pizza.

Pizza at Colonial was Dr. Jolly's answer for almost any threat to the fraternal order. But make no mistake, Jolly was the adult in the room. And he was the only one on the night of the Abbreviated Wrestling Match who foresaw the dangers of holding a major athletic event in the common room of a dormitory suite.

Ironically, it was Hyper, the third of the three sophomores across the hall, who cast the deciding vote that night. And not for the better for any of us, least of all himself. The name Hyper doesn't really do him justice. He was more than just the image next to the word "nerd" in the picture dictionary. Though he was all of that.

Hyper had a great appreciation for the ironies of life, and his eyes lit up like Times Square whenever he shared his observations about what he liked to call the "conundrums of campus life." Other times, however, he could work himself into a lather that was a sight to see. Anything could set him off. A poorly worded essay prompt, the tuna casserole at Wilcox dining hall, or the scratches on Clogs' *Houses of the Holy* album.

When the world failed to live up to his standards of grammatical construction, culinary refinement, or vinyl record care, he could get very animated. His voice would get pitchy, and he would lose his train of thought. That's when Clogs and Jolly, noting my alarm, would remind me, "He can get a little hyper." Often he would regain his composure and complete his thought.

At other times, his tongue would trip itself up, the color

would drain from his face, his eyes would bug out, and he sprayed like the Royal Shakespeare Company on opening night. He'd famously chant ominous phrases such as, "This is not good. This is not good. This is not good." Then he would finish with a tiny Edvard Munch infinite scream in a falsetto voice that sounded like Miles Davis playing with a Harmon mute on "'Round Midnight."

And that's not just me talking; Clogs and Jolly would describe it the same way.

The Butler's Table Did It

On the night of the Abbreviated Wrestling Match, we were hanging out waiting for inspiration when Clogs asked me if I wanted to wrestle. I shut him down with a firm, "No!"

Let me explain.

I hated wrestling going back to high school gym class. Pinning someone's shoulders to the ground until, all but paralyzed, they surrendered always seemed a little sadistic to me. And I often wondered what the rationale was for its being on the public school curriculum.

The thing I hated most was wrestling below my weight class. That happened when there weren't enough heavyweights to go around. It's a no-win situation for the person with more body mass. If I pinned my opponent, it was a big meh. Nobody roots for the bull. Conversely, if I was too rough with my opponent or appeared too proud after pounding him into submission, the gym would fill with hisses of disapproval.

I never knew what degree of force to use. This was a dilemma because if I dialed down the adrenaline too far and let my opponent execute so much as a simple escape, tales of dishonor would follow me around the public square like cuckoldry in a Lina Wertmüller movie.

Middle- and even lightweights were always challenging me to wrestle. Of course, they didn't really want to wrestle. They just wanted to start at the bottom of the referee's position and try out their escape moves that our Phys Ed teachers assured them could prevail even against larger opponents.

Their plan was to bust a sit-out and hip-heist, a head-and-arm Gazoni, or any number of escape combinations they'd been taught, and declare victory. If that didn't work, they would insist on a do-over. Eventually, you let them escape, just to end the whole miserable ordeal, and victory for them was no less sweet.

It was just such a scenario Clogs had in mind on the night of the Abbreviated Wrestling Match. "I don't think that's a good idea," Jolly said. That's when Hyper surprised us all. "I don't know. It could be *very* interesting." Hyper was a person of infinite curiosity. He really was.

After lengthy negotiations, I agreed to a "non-competitive demonstration event." Where I would offer "token resistance" so Clogs could "exhibit" his favorite move from, of course, the bottom of the referee's position.

"I have a bad feeling about this," Jolly insisted. Leaving Jolly's cautionary note aside, it may have been a harmless exercise in appeasement had there not been several best practices overlooked that evening. Beginning with, if you are going to wrestle in a crowded room, you should at least MOVE THE COFFEE TABLE.

Maybe it was the understated elegance of that brass-winged, Chippendale-style butler's table that made it easy to overlook the obvious threat it posed. Or maybe we were all too unimaginative to see how a simple kick-out and switch or a well-executed Granby roll is all it would take for Clogs to land his second lumbar vertebra squarely on its sharp hardwood corner.

And when he did, *"Pow! Blap! Bif! Zok!"* Bolts of pain shot from him like cheesy graphics in a comic book. His body went into a kind of fetal paralysis in the middle of the floor, where he remained silent and motionless for longer than one might imagine a still-live body in extreme pain could...especially one curled up on its back with its head, arms, and legs suspended in midair.

Jolly, Hyper, and I instinctively retreated to separate corners to create space for Clogs to writhe in pain should he ever regain motor control. An uncomfortable amount of time passed before we heard him make the first of a series of unnatural sounds.

Finally, catharsis came when he let out a string of f-bombs that wrapped around the highest spires of Princeton's Gothic architecture and sent the clapper in Nassau Hall's bell tower ringing. One long pulsing stream of interlocking luminescent f-bombs lit up the night sky and snaked its way around every monkey clown, literate ape, and chained dragon gargoyle on campus, where they remain in their dormant state to this day.

Spectacular as the Mercer County sky may have been that night, its pageantry paled in comparison with the f-bomb world records that Clogs set, including, the World's Loudest F-bomb, the World's Longest F-bomb, the Most Consecutive F-bombs. And one that had to be the funniest even if there is no real way to measure that sort of thing.

No sooner had Clogs completed his stream of invective than Hyper went into the dark and ominous phrase part of his act. "You hurt Clogs. You hurt Clogs. You hurt Clogs," and charged at me in an infinite rage. When his hands clutched for my throat, I planted my palms on his chest to break his advance. His knees buckled and his butt dropped into the chair behind him, his legs draped over its arms and feet dangling in midair.

His slapstick pratfall cut the tension in the room, and we all had a good long laugh. Even Clogs. "Well, that was pretty dumb," Hyper said, his acute sense of irony returning, as he rolled his eyes like Curly in *The Three Stooges* after a flowerpot falls on his head—but without the chorus of chirping birds.

Then, as if on cue, Jolly declared the verdict, "That was very strange." He threw his hands over his head and finished with the obligatory, "What the hell? Let's go to Colonial for a pizza!" We left Hyper sprawled in the chair, limbs akimbo, with a "*nyuk-nyuk-nyuk*" grin on his face while we went out for pizza and beer.

The Colonial Restaurant was our favorite haunt that year. As best as I can recall, all you could get there was pitchers of pilsner and plain pizza pies. I don't think they even had a menu. You just sat down, and they brought you the next pie out of the oven and the next pour from the tap. Whether you wanted it or not.

Anyway, we had fun recounting the highlights of the Abbreviated Wrestling Match over some 'za and suds. And the irony was not lost on us that Hyper had gotten more upset with the evening's events than Clogs. Of course, we all knew he could get a little hyper.

When we returned to 1915 Hall, Einstein was climbing out our dorm-room window. Naturally, we asked him why he was climbing out the window. He told us Hyper tried to crash our door with a set of barbells that no one even knew he had. But, as I tried to explain in the Case of the Purloined Grocery Cart, he only managed to jam the lock. "He's very mad at Al," Einstein cautioned. "And he mentioned something about a lawsuit."

The Duel in West College

The next morning, I got a call from the dean of student affairs, and I could tell right away he didn't want to fill me in on the history of Princeton football. Though he had some knowledge about the night of the Abbreviated Wrestling Match that I didn't know, such as how Hyper checked himself into the McCosh infirmary for a sedative and overnight care. He then presented his medical records to the dean as evidence that I was a danger to the student body, along with his recommendation for expulsion.

I gave the dean my side of the story about the Abbreviated Wrestling Match, though I didn't go all the way back to the dago/Jew stuff. Some people are touchy about such things. For all I knew, the Dean might have been one of them. I did mention the unfortunate oversight regarding the butler's table, Hyper's mad rush at me, and the muted Edvard Munch infinite scream.

I suspect he already heard my version of the Abbreviated Wrestling Match from Clogs and Jolly, because he immediately asked me how I was doing. I told him I was fine, although I found myself periodically glancing over my shoulder checking for rear-guard action from Hyper. And I thought I might be developing a tic.

The dean shared some comforting thoughts about the constructive nature of remorse and how it is not inextricably tied to guilt, and I was feeling like I might wiggle out of this one like I did in the Case of the Purloined Grocery Cart. Then we agreed a meeting with Hyper might help clear the air.

The next day, the three of us met in the dean's cavernous office. It was so large that it looked like it could have been a courtroom back when West College was built in 1836. Hyper and I sat in green leather chairs against opposite walls that were separated by enough space to hold a duel should anyone during the Van Buren administration choose pistols as their preferred method of dispute resolution.

Of course, there is nothing in the historical record to suggest that flintlocks were ever fired in West College. Weehawken was New Jersey's preferred dueling ground at the time. However, the room was so immense I couldn't help but imagine that something like that might have been on the architect's mind when he was drawing up his plans.

The dean sat behind his desk along an adjacent wall, strategically placed, I suspected to remain out of the line of fire. I was still rehearsing my opening statement when the dean started the meeting. It lasted no longer than it took Alexander Hamilton and Aaron Burr to walk ten paces, turn, and fire.

When the dean characterized the Abbreviated Wrestling Match as an unfortunate accident, Hyper knew he had lost the narrative. That's when he went into a near-perfect historical reenactment of the events of the night in question.

When with ample room between us to reach full attack speed, he rose from his seat and dashed towards me. Eyes bugged, hands clutching for my throat, spraying like Brando in *Streetcar*, "This is not good. This is not good. This is not good." Exactly as I had described it to the Dean the day before.

Only the Emmy Award–nominated writers of the popular CBS legal drama *Perry Mason* could shamelessly suggest such an ending to a courtroom scene. But that's how it happened. And that's how I got my single room in Pyne Hall.

Exile

After the duel in West College, nobody bothered to tell me about my new housing arrangements until I returned to my dorm where Clarence the Proctor was waiting outside. He didn't look at all surprised that we should meet again under such door-damaged circumstances.

A small university truck pulled up. Proctor Clarence and the driver exchanged pleasantries as I passed my belongings out the window to him one stereo component, crate of records, and Glad bag of blue jeans at a time. After all my stuff was loaded, they shuttled me off to exile in Pyne Hall.

That evening at about ten o'clock, I closed my textbook for my nightly study break. It was my custom to head to the Wilcox Hall vending machines for a can of hot Dinty Moore Beef Stew. It was a bit of a trek from my new pad at Pyne to the now out-of-the-way Wilcox, but I didn't know where else I could find hot beef stew in a can at that time of night.

Part of my regular routine was running into Dudsy on a Bachman Pretzel Stix run. We would take our vending machine plunder upstairs to the TV room where Ersatz Cowboy Joel would be watching highlights of the Senate Watergate Committee proceedings and practicing his katas.

I knew the additional ground I had to cover could throw off the timing I needed to hit my marks with Dudsy and Ersatz. So, I really hoofed it until I reached the hill overlooking the tennis courts. There I saw the lights of 1915 Hall, shining like a beacon ahead. And I got that warm, almost-home feeling.

Just then, the window to my former dormitory room cracked open and a boot appeared, followed by a leg. And then a second boot, followed by a second leg. Soon, Einstein's torso and head followed. After clearing the sill and jambs, he dropped the remaining three feet to the ground below.

I was happy to see him because he was a good guy. That Mahler and *State Fair* thing didn't bother me so much after I got to know him. And by then, I was used to hearing stuff like "my dad worked with Einstein." It was no big deal if you think of it. I mean, it wasn't like his dad *was* Einstein.

I was about to call out when Hyper appeared.

And I realized that so long as Hyper was still around, I could never go to Wilcox Hall—or anywhere in Wilson College—again. It was like a whole chunk of campus collapsed in on itself taking the Dinty Moore vending machines along with it, leaving a gaping, smoldering hole in the middle of campus, and my life. I would have to navigate around this loss forever. And I would need a new study-break food source.

"Man, living in a single as a first year really sucks," I thought.

My Dark Adventure with the Billboard Hot 100

A few weeks later, I was walking through Blair Arch to McCosh Hall and heard Clogs' favorite refrain. "Hey, how'd your dago?" I knew my life had cratered when I felt my spirits rise at the sound of those words. Yet, I didn't reciprocate with my obligatory antisemitic rejoinder. Which, of course, was not meant to offend him.

We chatted briefly and he told me that Hyper left the university to "get real" for a while. Hyper said he would return in the fall or maybe transfer somewhere else. He wasn't sure. And then Clogs, in a rare moment of sincerity said, "It wasn't you; it was coming on for a while. It's for the best."

The B-Side of Paradise

There might have been a time when Clogs' words of absolution would have lifted my spirits. But I was already in a mental battle with Roberta Flack's Grammy Award–winning Record of the Year—that hit number one on the Billboard Hot 100 on February 24, 1973, and remained there for five excruciating weeks.

The concurrence of the endless stream of miserable events in my first year with the crest of popularity of Flack's paean to psychic pain brought me as close to a state of clinical depression as I have ever known. If that sounds hyperbolic, let me remind you about Pi-Man, the Mayor of Baltimore, the vast chain of disdain, Fritz Crisler's winged helmet, the Case of the Purloined Grocery Cart, and the stupid wrestling match that I never should have agreed to in the first place.

Even with all that, my dark adventure with the Billboard Hot 100 might have been avoided if my morning DJ understood that songs about despair are no way to start a day. Not to diss Roberta Flack— a huge talent, who possesses what I believe singers call "a great instrument." And is rumored to be a beautiful person inside and out. But "Killing Me Softly with His Song" is just not a morning song. Especially for someone in the state I was in.

Over time, if I haven't already mentioned, it made me question life itself.

Until one day when I was lying on my back in bed, staring at the dappled plaster ceiling above, and I succumbed to the popular zeitgeist. At first, by silently mouthing its words. Then, paying full-throated homage to the song's structural integrity. And belting out each word of Roberta Flack's RIAA Certified Gold single like a singular cry for help until...

I heard a *rap-tap-tap* on my door. I scraped myself off the bed, beat myself with a stick over to the door, and opened it.

The Abbreviated Wrestling Match

"Are you all right in here?"

"Yeah. I'm. I'm fine."

"Okay. Well… My name is Mark. I live across the hall. If you need anything."

"Thanks, Mark."

That's when I knew I had to make a change in my life.

The Space Between
the Legs of the Chair

The summer after graduation, I enrolled in a video work-shop with Ed Emshwiller, a cover illustrator for science fiction magazines and paperbacks with titles such as: *World Without Men, Threshold of Eternity,* and *Warlord of Kor.* He was also a pioneer in experimental films and video. His 1979 *Sunstone,* a short 3-D computer-generated video is part of the Museum of Modern Art's permanent collection. Ed was, as everyone in the class agreed and the reader may surmise, one tripped-out dude.

One day, for reasons known only to himself, he decided to share his observations with the class about the way my mind works. "If you ask someone to describe a chair," he began, "they might say 'a chair has four legs, a seat, and a back.' Ask Al the same question," he continued, "and he will describe the space around the chair and between its four legs."

My classmate's found this very amusing. I did, too... until I discovered how closely it resembled the Mayo Clinic's definition of schizophrenia. In the end, I chose to view his musings as a badge of honor that someone with as unconventional a mind as his could be so fascinated with mine. That said, to this day I peek under the old dome from time to time just to see how it is doing. But I have never found myself contemplating the space between the legs of a chair, sofa, divan or any other kind of seating. Until now.

The Remarkable Unknown Tiger

When I was researching this book, I googled "Remarkable Princetonians," and the top search result was the Wikipedia page "List of Princeton University People." There I found a catalog of about 650 historically significant alumni, all standouts in their fields of academia, government, arts and literature, math and science, sports, and business.

Even astronauts. No less than seven Tigers (including Pete Conrad, the third person to walk on the moon) have braved the final frontier. Even more if you count Jeff Bezos who thumbed a ride in 2021 on his company Blue Origin's flight into outer space. Although in the Federal Aviation Administration's record books Bezos goes down as a "spaceflight participant." A call Old Beez has always considered, "Harsh."

However, in reviewing this record of Tiger movers and shakers, I found myself thinking about the ones who didn't receive Pulitzer Prizes and MacArthur Fellowships, or become bank presidents, major generals, and moon-walkers—the unknown Tigers; the space between the legs of the chair.

Extrapolating from a 2008 article in the *Princeton Alumni Weekly*, there are about 135,000 students who have graduated from the school first known as the College of New Jersey since 1764. After deducting the "Wiki 650," that leaves 134,350 Tigers who toiled their mortal lives away in relative, if not complete, obscurity. Or, put another way, there are about 650 people over the past 270 years who make up the chair that is Princeton. And the rest of us occupy the historical space around them.

These are the people who interest me. The ones who didn't make it past the velvet rope and into the Wikipedia Ring of Honor. No doubt, many of them are remarkable human beings who have made their friends and loved ones proud. Surely, they all deserve recognition.

I have a story about one who does. Someone who is unforgivably unknown. So unknown that *I* don't even know who he is. Which is why I call him the Remarkable Unknown Tiger. His story begs to be told, however, not because of his lack of notoriety but because of his remarkable acts of kindness. To me. While technically the protagonist here, I remind you that I don't know who he is. Fittingly, his part in this narrative will be spare. Though mine won't.

Back to Me

Every day for a period of five weeks, beginning in late February of my first year, I woke to the sounds of Roberta Flack's hit record "Killing Me Softly with His Song." It was a little ditty that made me (if I have failed to communicate this effectively) question life itself. That is, until one morning, dispirited from a year of one-too-many painfully eventful evenings, Ms. Flack beat me into a shapeless mass of insecurity and self-doubt. And I decided to make a change.

Reaching deep into that endless reservoir of hope and optimism, that only a Happy Bottom could muster, I picked myself up by my bootstraps, walked to Jadwin Gymnasium, and signed up for the first-year's baseball team. Some readers, remembering how things turned out the last time I joined an NCAA sports team, may be thinking, "Oh, no. Here we go, again."

But baseball was different. For me, it was a sure thing. And my desire to get back on track with accomplishments outside the classroom that would steel me against the vicissitudes of life as one of Princeton's pigs to the academic slaughter was strong.

Besides, baseball was a game that truly fit my psychological profile. First, it is physically undemanding, as sports go. For instance, if you've never played it, ninety percent of the time, the most aerobic thing you are called on to do is jog to and from the dugout to your position in the field at the beginning and end of each inning. If you are fortunate enough to play first base, like I was, that meant a very short trip, especially at home games.

Better still, once you're in the field, all you do is kick the dirt around on the infield for ten minutes, spit, then return to the dugout and hang out with your friends. There, on the dugout bench, you can make fun of the opposing pitcher's funny sideburns or unorthodox wind-up and otherwise engage in saucy banter. Basically, baseball is a game you can play while smoking a pack of cigarettes. Which, I believe, is why they call it the great national pastime.

Of course, from time to time you are called on to roll your Marlboros up in your uniform sleeve, cut the saucy banter, and walk to home plate to meet your fate. Where, in a 21-square-foot, two-dimensional rectangle outlined in white chalk called the batter's box, you remain until history declares you a winner or a loser.

The B-Side of Paradise

As if awaiting the verdict of history isn't bad enough, hitting a baseball is hard. After calculating the speed of a pitched baseball and the distance it travels, a batter has a mere quarter second to decide whether to swing or not. And then you must swing in exactly the right place.

Hitting a baseball is widely considered the toughest thing to do in any sport. It's a well-worn phrase that even the best hitters fail seventy percent of the time. Commendably, the baseball rule book reflects the heavy psychological toll the batter's box can take by allowing you to call time out if things get too stressful.

Once permission is granted, you can step out of the box to get your head straight. Considering that an average at bat lasts under two minutes, baseball's charitable batter's box sick-leave policy remains one of the most progressive mental health accommodations in American life.

So important is hitting to the game that it is baseball dogma that if you hit, you play. Guess what made baseball a sure path to my salvation? I could hit! I mean, I could tear the cover off the ball. I was so good that it was the subject of my greatest revelation during that phase of life we call the midlife crisis.

"It is a sobering thought," I said to myself in one of those man-in-the-mirror moments we all have soon after blowing out fifty candles on the cake, "that I have never been as good at any aspect of life than I was at hitting a baseball."

Imagine the gravity of such a statement that covers a vast expanse of human endeavors. From algebra to coloring inside the lines, brushing my teeth, all those things I had to do as a magazine publisher, husband, father, and friend—or even working the remote control on the television. I could never perform a magic trick, play the guitar, or bake a souffle.

The Space Between the Legs of the Chair

And I always forget something from the cleaning supplies aisle when my wife sends me to the grocery store.

Considering that hitting a baseball was a skill I had mastered by the age of nine, the next forty-one years of my life could be fairly described as a period of low personal growth.

Oddly enough, it was a trip to the optometrist that triggered this self-reflection. Somewhere between the visual acuity and the visual refraction tests, my optometrist asked me if I had ever been a baseball player. "I bet you were a good hitter," she said.

"Why do you ask?"

"You have twenty/ten vision," I heard her say, not knowing that such a thing even existed. "We call them baseball player's eyes."

What that means is: I could see details at twenty feet that people with 20/20 vision can only see at ten. A huge advantage in the split-second world of hitting. Of course, this only served to feed my midlife despair. As I could now see how all the virtues I had associated with my ability to hit a baseball were part of a false narrative. Another example of describing the space between the legs of the chair instead of the legs themselves....

To understand what I mean, let's consider the great Boston Red Sox hitter Dustin Pedroia. Sportscasters regularly equated Pedroia's batting skill with some of humanity's most exemplary traits. He was said to be a "smart hitter," "disciplined at the plate," and "a real battler," all measures of character that are respected and valued.

Pedroia's "strength of character" was an inspiration to Little Leaguers the world over and was fallaciously lauded by sportswriters as a testament to how willpower can overcome physical limitations as Pedroia stood just five-foot-nine.

Fully five inches shorter than the average major leaguer. But the sportswriters were using the wrong metric. Height is not the legs of a baseball batter's chair, his eyes are. Pedroia could hit because he had 20/10 vision. He was not the virtuous man; he was an optical genetic freak.

More About the Remarkable Unknown Tiger

All this was necessary to explain why my new plan (to get my Happy Bottom back in gear) could not fail. It also provides a framework within which the Remarkable Unknown Tiger's (the protagonist of this story) remarkable acts took place.

Back to Me

I suspect the Remarkable Unknown Tiger witnessed my most remarkable demonstration of hitting prowess—that singular endeavor, without which my life has had no value. It was at the Jadwin Gymnasium batting cage where the team practiced when it rained. A large target hung above the pitching machine. A reminder to all that hitting the ball in the middle of the field delivers the most productive results.

Hitting that target was not easy. Even the best players on the team struggled to hit it twice, maybe three times in ten pitches. One day, I put all ten pitches inside that circle. That's what the baseball cognoscenti call "locked in."

To mentally lock in, according to PurposefullLife.com, is to never quit; to embrace challenges, practice hard work, and have heart. That's the same kind of character-affirming gobbledygook I was trained to believe about myself, until my optometrist decided to get chatty with me. And I discovered that my core competency was merely a vision thing.

Another benefit of my visual superpower was the advantage it lent in reading a depth chart, where I noticed, no doubt from a greater distance than players with 20/20 vision, that I was at the bottom. So lost was I in the reverie of my batting stroke that spring, I never took note of whether the coach even knew my name.

I soon found out, when I paid him a visit, that he did not. I was sure he had accidentally transposed my player evaluation with somebody else's. And all I had to do was help him align my name with the correct appraisal on his chart and we would be good to go. Imagine my dismay when I realized early on in our conversation that there were no player evaluations and there was no chart.

"You're a leftie?" he asked.

"Nope."

When I explained that he was mistaking me for someone else, he folded his lips into a man purse and rubbed the stubble on his chin. Audibly. The instantly recognizable sign that somebody doesn't know who the hell you are. And wishes it could have remained that way.

Over to the Twilight Zone

This brings us back, as things often do in my life, to the *Twilight Zone*. Specifically, the episode "To See the Invisible Man." A story that envisions a future society where certain crimes are punished by social shunning. People are sentenced to invisibility for a year, and each receives an implant on their forehead as a warning to others to see and steer clear. After serving a year of invisibility himself, a man named Mitchell hugs an "invisible" woman because he is touched by her pleas to be noticed. Something this phantom first baseman needed desperately at that time.

And Back to Me

When the team took the practice field that afternoon, the still-stubbled coach divided us into two squads for a scrimmage—another one of those "depth-chart-challenges" that I had seen before on the football field the previous fall, where I might dig myself out of a hole.

In my first at bat, I hit a single to right field. It was not exactly a work of art. In the vernacular of baseball, it is called a "dying quail"—a soft looper that lands without fanfare in the mid-outfield. But a hit is a hit. And I took solace in the fact that by the time I came to bat for the second time, it was still the only one in the game.

This time I hit what they call a "frozen rope" that fishtailed over the center fielder's head. It whipped back in a parabolic curve, like the tail of a fish when it's trying to escape a hook. It was a beauty that sent the center fielder into a comedic spill, his legs twisting under him as he tried to complete a 360-degree turn to follow the flight of the ball. This was one you stuff and hang over the fireplace.

Coach Stubble (how could I resist?) having seen enough abruptly called off the scrimmage where I now possessed all its two hits. And I felt confident that I was invisible no more.

That Saturday, the seemingly chastened Stubble had me

take batting practice with the starters before the first game of our double-header against Montclair State. This meant I could expect some action, even if only as a pinch hitter, and maybe get a start in the second game.

It was one of those bone-chilling March days that remind you why major league teams take preseason training in Florida. It was the kind of day when batters go to the plate hoping to draw a walk rather than having to hit the ball. This is because if you don't have a tight grip on the bat handle, you can get a painful sting in your hands when (god forbid) your bat makes contact with the ball—a sting that travels up your arms to the pain matrix in your brain and from there down through all your vital organs until it reaches your bowels… and remains for days.

I fought that fear back through five hours of Arctic freeze. Waiting for my chance to unleash my magnificent 20/10s on any sorry-ass pitcher they conspired to throw against me. In the final inning of the second game, with two outs and two strikes on the last batter, and the cold breath of late winter bitch-slapping me like the pathetic benchwarmer I had become, the less chastened than I had imagined Stubble launched his devilish plan. First to freeze me out and then stick the dagger in. "D'Alessandro," he said calling my name as if he dared me to make lemonade out of the lemons he was serving, "grab a bat. Get up there and hit."

If you think this part of our story ends happily, you have been watching too many Hollywood movies. For those who don't appreciate just how unorthodox it is for a coach to call for a pinch hitter after a batter already has two strikes, find someone who knows that "the flip" is associated with Derek Jeter and the "October error" refers to Bill Buckner. They will tell you just how skeevy Stubble's maneuver was.

A few days later, opportunity knocked again when our starting first baseman broke his nose on a high hopper during infield practice. And our next-in-line first sacker pulled his hamstring running out to replace him. So, I grabbed my glove and hustled out to take infield practice.

Infield practice is a pregame drill where the coach hits a round of ground balls to the infielders who throw to the first baseman, who relays the ball to the catcher. And then you start again. The idea is to allow everyone to find their fielding rhythm and loosen up their arms. It is conducted at three-quarter speed because you're not actually trying to throw a runner out—it's just a warmup.

On the second round, the now clearly unchastened Stubble asked me to throw to third base instead of the catcher. Often called the most difficult throw in baseball, as a precaution, third basemen are taught to ease into it in warmups by starting at the pitcher's mound and slowly moving back a few paces with each successive toss until their arm is ready for the full cross-field throw.

Properly warmed up or not—and I wasn't—it was an unorthodox request because first basemen throw to third almost never. In fact, first basemen don't have to throw the ball much at all. Which is why the focus of infield drills is on warming up the other players' arms.

Over to Billy Beane

Don't take my word for it. Take it from Billy Beane, the legendary general manager who, by using the statistical methods of sabermetrics, led the Oakland Athletics to four consecutive playoff appearances and two American League Championship

Series, despite having one of the lowest payrolls in baseball.

Billy Beane's story was brought to the screen in the critically acclaimed 2011 movie *Moneyball* starring Brad Pitt, Jonah Hill, and Philip Seymour Hoffman. The relevant story in the movie is that of Scott Hatteberg, a washed-up catcher with irreversible nerve damage to his throwing arm.

Billy Beane likes Hatteberg because he has a high career on-base average at the plate, a statistic highly valued in sabermetrics. And because he can get him cheap, since every other general manager has already written him off as damaged goods.

In one of the movie's memorable scenes, Billy goes to Hatteberg's house to offer him a contract. A grateful but incredulous Hatteberg thanks Billy and reminds him that he can't throw. "That's okay," Billy says. "We'll stick you at first base." Had *Moneyball* made it to the screen forty years earlier, I might not be writing this story today.

And Back to Me

Choosing to ignore the low bar a first basemen's arm skills must clear, Stubble revealed just how unchastened (and arguably unhinged) he had become by insisting that I make a perfect throw to third base. My first hurl was decent, if imperfect. So, he made me throw over again. "Get it down!" I got it down. "At the ankles." I got it down at the ankles. "Not the left side of the bag. The right." The better my throws became, the greater his demands.

After a mind-numbing series of attempts, the, in my mind, exacting to a fault Stubble was still not satisfied that he could count on me to make a throw that I had only made once before in my baseball career—and then I was scolded for making it. As it is generally considered a high-risk/low-reward attempt at throwing out a runner that should be avoided.

Eventually, as these things go, I felt a pull in the back of my arm. I knew if I showed any sign of pain, I was toast. But he was too good. "Did you hurt your arm? I can't play you if you can't throw." Then the demon Coach Stubble, bowing his head as if it was a sad moment in baseball history akin to Lou Gehrig's Farewell speech, motioned someone else to first base. Anyone. It didn't matter. Because you can always stick anyone on first base.

I returned to the bench and waited for the lineup card to be handed to the umpire. Once I was officially out of the lineup, I took a slow and decidedly dramatic stroll to Jadwin Gymnasium, until I disappeared from their lives forever.

Inside the locker room, I removed my uniform for the last time. Each article of clothing slipped to the floor from its own weight onto a pile in the middle of the locker room floor. A double-knit monument to the complete unraveling of my high-school identity during my first year at college.

The Remarkable Unknown Tiger's Shining Moment

Nine months later, the captain of the varsity baseball team knocked on my door. With the formality the occasion might command in a Hollywood movie, he invited me on behalf of the coach and the players to join the team. "I would love to," I told him, like Scott Hatteberg to Billy Beane, "but I can't throw."

The Space Between the Legs of the Chair

How did the varsity coach hear about the Phantom First Baseman? And who, to paraphrase Daryl Strawberry, was the straw that stirred this drink? None other, of course, than our protagonist, the Remarkable Unknown Tiger, who shared my story directly.

The first claim he has to the legs of the Great Princeton Chair was his heart. Imagine the empathy and the courage required to knock on the door of the powers that be when you are just a rookie yourself, to advocate on behalf of someone you don't know—and when there is no benefit to you. It was the real-life equivalent of Mitchell's hug to the invisible woman whose pleas to be noticed couldn't be ignored in the *Twilight Zone* episode "To See the Invisible Man."

His second claim was his power of persuasion. Consider the rhetorical load he shouldered in trying to convince the coach that what Tiger baseball really needed was some lone wolf who befriended no one on the team when he had the chance and was last seen walking off the field without explanation after the first pitch of the Trenton State game roughly a year before. Now, *that's* remarkable.

For daring to see the Phantom First Baseman, I hereby nominate the Remarkable Unknown Tiger for induction on the Wiki 650. In my book, he is an integral part of the great chair that is Princeton. Whoever he is. Let's call him Mitchell. Thanks for noticing, Mitch. Thanks for the hug.

Sometimes I think Rod Serling has way too much influence over my life.

The
Rise

The Boy in the Bathroom

If one man's meat is another man's poison, then our Gentleman's Pipe Club of Hamilton Hall was an *Animal House* to the Boy in the Bathroom. At least that's what I came to understand on yet another eventful evening in my sophomore year.

There must have been something about our very existence that upset him. Our aura, our ambience, our spirit. Because, as I will demonstrate beyond a reasonable doubt, it wasn't anything we did or said to or about him. The truth is we were a stodgy foursome. Docile chair potatoes to a fault. Whose presence was felt beyond our walls only by the herbaceous aromatherapies we generously shared with everyone on our hall.

Furthermore, if the worst thing Bluto, Otter, Boon, and Pinto ever did was to overplay Bob Dylan's *Planet Waves* (at conversational volume), Jon Landis wouldn't have had much of a movie. Yet, traumatized by us the Boy in the Bathroom was. And one night the Office of the Dean of Undergraduate Students (ODUS) decided to find out why.

The B-Side of Paradise

It was a typical night when the Pipe Club was in session. Seated to my right was the wizardly Dudsy, my connection to the other members of the club who were friends from the lightweight football team. Lightweight, in this instance, referring to league weight limits imposed on its players. Not their intellectual capacity. Or their propensity to toss their suds far too soon.

Dudsy, as anyone who knew him would agree, couldn't traumatize a fly. As previously noted, he was a gentleman and a scholar whose theories on the Great Princeton Lab Experiment are still studied by sociologists and college administrators to this day. Or so he tells me.

Over to his right and continuing around a circle of club chairs frayed in all the right places, was Harry: the patriarch of the club. It was Harry's hand-carved Old Army briar-wood tobacco pipe that set the tone for the group's stately demeanor. It imbued within us a generosity of spirit that should have placed us above suspicion in the case of the Boy in the Bathroom.

Old Army was a gentleman's pipe, the kind a banker or a general in the armed forces might smoke. It lit the face and mind of anyone who held it, and it was a prevailing part of our nightly club activities to pass Old Army around to everyone in the circle. A testament to the good cheer and enduring character of its owner.

To my left, was Tom. If he taught me one thing, it was that it's good to have a preppy on your team. Tom, if you can imagine, was the impossible spawn of Barney Rubble and Thurston Howell III. At once a regular Joe and an heir to one of America's greatest family fortunes at the time.

Nothing says noblesse oblige like the enthusiasm he held for the hit CBS television series *Kojak*, starring the late, great

The Boy in the Bathroom

Telly Savalas. Without endlessly citing his signature line, "Who loves ya, baby?" Though when he did, it never failed to entertain.

Tom was the keeper of Old Army's flame. He nurtured that briarwood beauty like it was the Olympic Torch itself. From morning to night, when official club activities began, he kept that symbol of peace, friendship, and hope lit as if international harmony itself depended on it. This is the most tactful way I can think of to explain what needs to be said, that Tom was a stoner.

Yet, true to his station, he never betrayed the respectable image our club and the university so assiduously tried to maintain. If by midday his brain resembled a R. Crumb cartoon, on the outside he was always clear-eyed and fresh. Thanks to the trusty bottles of Visine and Binaca spray he always kept by his side. A pro move from a class guy.

Even at dinnertime, Tom would maintain his vigil. While Harry, Dudsy, and I were off grubbing it up in fine fashion and hobnobbing with high-tone people at the Holder Commons dining hall, Tom would remain behind. Working his single-burner Proctor Silex hot plate, preparing family-sized cans of Chef Boyardee Beefaroni or Chun King Chicken Chow Mein—and keeping Old Army lit.

It was a rare occasion when Tom would break from his self-appointed watch and join us at dinner. Once we confronted him on his antisocial behavior and he told us with all sincerity, and a complete lack of self-awareness, "I don't really like the food at Commons."

At other times, Tom could remind you how much the words of Old Fitz rang true when he wrote in "The Rich Boy," a short story he published in 1926: "... the very rich. They are different from you and me." For example, the impossible "dog ate my homework" story I overheard him telling one day.

"Hello, Bhikkhu?"

I could tell Tom immediately regretted using the club's nickname for our Buddhism professor, Bob Taylor, when a more formal one would have been in order. But the preppy in him powered on.

"My name is Tom, and I'm in your Religion 420 class." Then, by way of explaining why he hadn't made it to class yet, Tom asked for an extension on his midterm paper. "I've been out of town quite a bit this semester..." he began. As if in his spare time he was running field operations for the Fortune 500 company that bore his family name.

Tom understood as mere mortals never could, that "out of town" for seven weeks is an excuse so rarely found in the annals of Ivy League slacker lore, that few professors would have ever heard it. And if they had, no faculty member, including ODUS himself, would challenge anyone precocious enough to try it. Besides, matters like class attendance didn't faze Bhikkhu Bob who was otherwise engaged on the eightfold path to the cessation of suffering.

Still, it was a device that would never—could never— have crossed my mind. As "out of town" in my family was something done once a year when school was not in session. Sometimes, as in the case of our famed Atlantic City Turnaround, even then it could be all too brief to mention.

"Due last week, you say? Well, that's embarrassing. Where *does* the time go?"

As things would have it, we were gathered around the smoker's circle that eventful ODUS evening for our regular mid-week Buddhism 420 meditation—a course maligned by some as a cheap date on the otherwise high-minded courtship that is a liberal arts education. Largely because its only required reading was *The Dhammapada*, a book described by its U.S. publisher as a "collection of simple verses."

But one Tiger's shameful "gut" was another's stroll down the Noble Eightfold Path. And to those of us on the fast track to the true nature of reality, Homer and Shakespeare seemed needlessly dense. And don't even get me started on James Joyce.

Even the most sacred text of Theravada Buddhism, however, couldn't prepare us for the dean of undergraduate students paying us an unexpected visit on a Saturday night. The dean (who we will call Wormer because under the circumstances it would be impossible to call him anything else) carried a lined legal pad under his arm with a list of questions that by all appearances he was prepared to ask. Along with ample space on the bottom of the page to record any relevant testimony he might obtain.

Bob Dylan's "On a Night Like This" from his *Planet Waves* album was playing (at conversational volume) when he arrived. And I remember thinking how perfectly the song, that depicted an evening of great reminiscences with an old flame, captured the moment. Because ODUS opened with a series of disarming questions, as if this would be a folksy visit from a good friend from your past.

"How do you like Princeton?" "How are your classes going?" "Have you picked a major yet?" He even asked how we liked the food at Commons. And of course, no one spoke more enthusiastically about the quality of Commons food than Tom. Preppies just instinctively know how to play authority figures.

It isn't common for ODUS to show up at your door on a weekend night, so I figured it must be a welcome wagon visit that all students get sooner or later. Less clear was why it was happening in sophomore year, rather than being part of the first-year orientation process… Still, I was impressed by the university's thoughtful, if belated, gesture.

However, the conversation assumed a different tone when the dean pulled out his pen and eyed us one at a time as he asked, "Have you ever noticed any improper behavior between students on the hall?" Even I could figure out this was turning into official ODUS business and was relieved that nobody had been pumping the keg and cursing the foam when he arrived.

If we presented any red flags at all, it would have to be the skunky, piney scent of cannabis that filled the air. Though it's worth mentioning there was nothing too *Up in Smoke* about the scene. We weren't disappearing in a comical Cheech and Chong pot cloud. Thanks to another of Old Army's virtues: its aluminum screen.

Club protocol was to lower Old Army's screen after each draw on the pipe, much as an English nobleman on a hunt might do after releasing the hounds. Thereby snuffing its embers before passing. Not so much for the obvious benefit of preventing all that hempy goodness from going up in smoke instead of into your lungs where it can do the most good but for our greater interest in conducting club business consistent with the image of the prestigious academic institution whose beneficences we enjoyed.

You see, it really was a gentleman's pipe.

On this night, however, even Old Army's screen couldn't damper the storm mounting in Wormer as he continued with his new and, I might add, somewhat discomforting line of questioning. "Everyone gets along?" "No friction?"

Tom stepped up and took control.

The Boy in the Bathroom

"As a matter of fact, we haven't noticed anything of the sort," he said. "Why do you ask?" Then he lifted Old Army's screen, fired it up, took a hit, and offered it to Wormer. A "not in our house" move for the ages.

That's when we detected a faint Wormer squirm that betrayed the dilemma he was in. For this was as much an existential moment for Wormer and the university as it was for us. Because Tom was not just any rich kid legacy of a major donor.

His father was a singularly important alumnus. Virtually every college textbook in the country passed through his very hands, and in him, every Princeton professor's mind-numbing study of the art of the Greek nude, reform in rural Russia, or boundary behavior of holomorphic functions found a willing publisher.

Further complicating the matter was the fact that The Boy in the Bathroom was a once-in-a-generation mathematical mind—and just twelve years old! Wormer, you see, was faced with a classic struggle between the interests of the university's brain trust and its endowment trust. One that no amount of training could prepare him for. It was a quintessential Hail Mary moment for an Ivy League dean. And I could tell by the way he was eyeing me that he was looking for a fall guy.

To understand the volumes the Wormer squirm spoke, imagine the day he received an urgent message, in the form of a handwritten note, reading simply: "irate dad on phone." On almost any other day, being the seasoned pro that he was, and it already being midafternoon, he might have held that call over to the next day, as he had a tight schedule that included a squash game at four and dinner with the university provost at Lahiere's at seven.

The B-Side of Paradise

But there was something in the way his assistant dotted her "i" and crossed her "t" that prompted him to take the call. That's when he learned that Bluto, Otter, Boon, and Pinto were loose in Hamilton Hall. And were traumatizing the twelve-year-old math prodigy who lived there. A student whose promise drew the attention of none other than the great Bilbo himself, who personally involved himself in recruiting him away from MIT.

Still unaware of the identities of the boys in Hamilton Hall's Suite 2A, Wormer wasn't sweating it yet. He had seen situations like this before. That's why, for symbolic reasons, he kept a hard hat in his office, lest anyone think he was incapable of administering tough love. Something he was fully prepared to rain down on the Delta Tau Chi guys who were working the child genius's nerves.

Standing up to practice his backhand, in a consummate Ivy League dean's version of "Don't worry. I got this," he reassured the boy's father that he would investigate the situation. On his way out of the office, Wormer requests a list of names of the residents in Hamilton Hall's Suite 2A from his assistant. He heads off to Dillon Gym for his squash game wondering if, later in the evening, the Chenin Blanc would pair well with the Coquilles Saint-Jacques.

The next morning, he discovers the identities of the boys in 2A, realizes the potential for embarrassment for the university, and wishes he hadn't followed up that dry light-bodied French white with the round mouthfeel with all those Hennessy XOs and Hoyo de Monterrey Double Coronas the night before.

On the other hand, playing devil's advocate as he was trained to do, he reminds himself that the boy told his father he "can't take it anymore." But was not forthcoming about what exactly he couldn't take. So, there may be no provocation at all; just normal college pressures amplified by the boy's tender age.

After allowing himself a moment to embrace this appealing storyline, the worst-case scenario begins to take shape in Wormer's over-active ODUS mind, flashing across it, as these things tend to do, like a chyron on the evening news:

"ODUS Misses Signs of Bullying—Math Prodigy Dead at Ivy League School."

This prompted him to take a trip to Hamilton Hall. On a Saturday night. Unannounced. To see for himself.

Tom, not to break protocol, passed Old Army to Harry after Wormer declined. Harry lifted the screen, relit the bowl, took a toke, and lowered it again as Wormer continued. "The reason I ask is because I want to make sure everyone is getting along." In a variety of ways from the spoken word to head and hand gestures, we assured him that everyone, indeed, gets along.

"You haven't noticed any taunting or teasing?"

"No taunting or teasing," Harry replied.

"No bullying?"

"Nothing like that," Dudsy said.

Then the dean looked at me because I hadn't said anything yet.

"And you?"

But it was hard staying focused on Wormer's exacting line of questioning with Dylan in the background singing about some big-boned gal named Tough Mama he wanted to… I don't know that's when ODUS interrupted me.

Fortunately, Tom (it's good to have a preppy on your team) bailed me out. "Did something happen?"

"That's what I'm trying to find out. You see, there's a boy living down the hall. I'm sure you know him. A young boy. Just twelve years old…"

And then, in yet another Emmy Award–winning resolution of a courtroom scene, I exclaimed, "There's a *twelve-year-old boy* living down the hall?"

That silenced the crowd. But no measure of disbelief in my roommate's or Wormer's eyes could keep me from continuing my own line of cross-examination.

"*Why* is there a twelve-year-old boy living down the hall?"

"He's a student here," Harry explained.

"He's a *student* here?"

"You know, the boy who wears a bathing suit in the shower."

Tom, Dudsy, and Harry all tried to jog my memory with images of the Boy in the Bathroom—in the bathroom. But nothing worked. I had no awareness of having a preadolescent hall-mate two doors down. No matter what his sartorial preferences were.

"I'm sorry," I said. "I don't *really* notice what people wear in the shower."

Even Wormer had a laugh at that. Tom, Dudsy, and Harry joined him, and they all had a good time at my expense before I offered my final cross question, "Well, how long has he been living there?"

Ever so subtly, Wormer's wiry frame dropped deeper into his chair as he came to the realization, with what surely had to be a mix of relief and disappointment, that there would be no quick fix to the problem of the Boy in the Bathroom. Rather, what lay in store was a protracted period of hand-holding with the boy's father until faith could be restored. Until then, there would be no further late nights at Lahiere's.

Tucking his legal pad under his arm and returning his pencil to his jacket pocket, Wormer signaled that the case was closed. What he had here was another example of first-year culture shock. And the only thing left for Wormer to do was to deputize us on his behalf.

"Thanks, for your help, boys. Do me a favor, tread lightly. He's young and having a difficult adjustment to college. If you see anyone teasing him in any way, please let me know."

We all assured him he could count on us. And as Wormer fully relaxed, perhaps for the first time that evening, we took pride in knowing that in some small way we had helped restore his faith in the Tiger student body.

That prompted Dudsy to fire up Old Army. And in a celebratory breach of protocol passed it to me without dropping the wind screen. I, in turn passed it to Tom who passed it to Harry—Wormer having declined a second time—and we kept that big bowl going for two full trips around the circle before we had to trash the ash and reload.

Wormer hung out with us for a while, and we all kicked back while he asked us more questions about life at Princeton. Like, if we were going to join an eating club. And what we did for fun on weekends. Although, I think he realized as soon as the words were out of his mouth, that he was witnessing it.

He finally ducked out at a quarter to ten and we immediately turned on the tube to catch the end of Murderers' Row. It was the only time all year that we missed CBS's epic Saturday night comedy lineup: *All in The Family*, *M*A*S*H*, the *Mary Tyler Moore Show*, and *The Bob Newhart Show*.

Tom was not happy about missing his weekly Lou Grant fix. Lou, being his second-favorite TV character after Kojak. But he never held Wormer's presumptuous intrusion against him because Tom understood, as only peerage can, that's what the simple folk do.

At precisely 9:58, after the button on *The Bob Newhart Show*, Harry, our Saturday night beer runner, leapt out the window, as he had done on every other Saturday night at this precise time, and sprinted the approximately 50 yards to Varsity Liquors to pick up a case of Rolling Rock pony bottles before it closed at ten.

Soon after that night, the Boy in the Bathroom's father moved into Hamilton Hall, and lived with his son in that tiny one-room single for the rest of the school year. We used to watch him leave in the morning with his suit on to go to work, and return in the evening, his tie loose at the neck from a hard day at the office. Other than that, he was completely inconspicuous. In fact, I don't think I ever saw him in the bathroom. Not even once.

Although wouldn't you know it, from that night on, I saw his son in there every morning. He had a nice leather toiletries kit and several solid-colored Speedo swim briefs. He might have had one with a print on it, I don't really remember. I don't pay much attention to those kinds of things.

Anyway, his dad's presence was a real game changer because the Boy in the Bathroom was no further trouble to us after that.

Two Remarkable Tigers

Even card-carrying *B-Siders* must admit that Princeton University has educated generations of remarkable students, many of which have made remarkable contributions to the world, such as the great twentieth-century political philosopher John Rawls, whose 1971 *A Theory of Justice* has informed our social and political thinking ever since. And Alan Turing, the mathematician famous for breaking the Enigma code that helped defeat Nazi Germany.

Further, it's more than a matter of trivia to note that Old Nassau's "Big Cat Training Institute" has groomed two United States Presidents, twelve Supreme Court Justices, more central bankers than you can shake a stick at, and seventy-nine Nobel Prize recipients. Mostly in Physics, which is a science, and Economics which is a joke.

Of course, all this is fine parlor talk for those who bow to conventional measures of success. Which I don't. Success being, to those who have never experienced it, the ultimate microaggression. What's more, these uber-achievers are the exact kind of mousers who ratchet up the stress levels for the larger population of stray cats on campus, unsettling those in the Princeton litter for whom the Ivy League is more a dasher of dreams than a springboard to fame and fortune.

With that in mind, allow me to rearrange the stripes on the Tiger with these heroic tales about a couple of remarkable cats I met while I was there.

Remarkable Tiger 1: Dan Reefer

Dan Reefer was an elite high-school STEM student and all-around great guy who had an encyclopedic knowledge of the best cannabis strains from Thailand, Afghanistan, Acapulco, Jamaica, and the Hawaiian Islands. Dan could pair the finest marijuana varietals with your desired mood the way a master sommelier pairs wines with food. He taught me the best weed to smoke on a sunny day or a rainy night, to combat stress or to gain focus. Or lose it.

The descendant of chieftains from the Onondaga Nation, from an admissions standpoint Dan was a royal flush. An elite Engineering School applicant and track star, Dan's file received two powerful special consideration tags as it shot its way up the admissions mail chute. Namely, the yellow athletic recruit tag. And the green, what was called at the time, "minority tag." Draw a hand like his in Vegas and you will be banned for life from every casino on the strip.

When the admissions committee opened his file, it was happy dance time on University Place. In those days, America's favorite happy dance was the Time Warp from *The Rocky Horror Picture Show*, whose most memorable step was an unrepentant pelvic thrust—a move the director of admissions herself busted on a tabletop that day upon reviewing Dan's application. With, according to Princeton admissions lore, rapture in her eyes and hips.

Of course, Dan's admissions file has no bearing on why he's on my nomination list for the Wiki 650. His credentials for me are simple: He was generous and wise, and I saw him perform the single greatest act of forgiveness in the history of the cat family, if not the entire animal kingdom. As you might suspect, I was its beneficiary. Adding to his legendary stature was his custom of speaking, at least to my ear, like the characters in a Hemingway novel.

"My name is Dan Reefer. And I'm a dealer," he said, choosing simple language for direct effect, when he walked into an official meeting of the Gentleman's Pipe Club of Hamilton Hall one afternoon. It was a grand entrance for the ages, leaving Tom, Dudsy, Harry, and me speechless. Until Tom (it's good to have a preppy on your team) had the presence of mind to stand up, shake his hand, and say, "It's nice to meet you, Dan. Would you care to join us?"

No doubt the reader is thinking the same thing we were thinking, "Is Dan Reefer really his name?" And while we all wanted to ask, no one could quite get the words out. Nor did he address the question that surely had to be on the minds of every person in every room he ever invited himself into under similar circumstances. We could not have been the first to wonder how it came to be that his surname so closely matched his chosen occupation.

"I noticed your cannabis smoke while passing your window. So, I let myself in." And then, in a Tony Award–winning display of theatrical stagecraft, we responded in unison, "And *we're* glad you did!"

After that, the lines wrote themselves. "You can call me if you ever need good weed," he said.

"We *always* need good weed, Dan." He nodded and rolled a joint.

"I call this Lion's Weed. It is uplifting and relaxing with no mental cloudiness. A good fall afternoon weed." By the time he left, several sticks later, he had cleaned out all four of our checking accounts and every penny we could find between the couch cushions.

In the days ahead, Reefer taught me the differences between sativa and indica strains of marijuana—and why I needed to know them. For instance, sativa has long, thin leaves; is THC dominant; and gives you a head high. It is uplifting and euphoric and increases energy and alertness. It's best for daytime use. Indica weed has shorter and wider leaves, is CBD dominant, and provides a body high. It is the better nighttime choice—great for kicking back and listening to music or using as a sleep aid.

He even told me he could recommend some weed that is *very* high in THC content that can make you *very* paranoid.

"Why would I want to make myself *very* paranoid, Reef?"

And in a line whose inspiration could only be the conversations of Jake Barnes and Lady Brett Ashley from *The Sun Also Rises*, he explained, "Because some people like that."

Reef was one crazy Tiger Town cat… He was so free of the traditional worries of life that he used recreational drugs to experience what it's like to *not* be at peace with himself. "If you don't like unexplained fears," he cautioned, "you will want to avoid South American weed."

That spring, the Beach Boys came to town for what was the biggest concert of the year. Campus music lovers had already enjoyed a banner lineup of acts such as Philip Glass and Keith Jarrett selling out the 900-seat Alexander Hall, and Tom Waits and Steve Goodman selling out the 1,100-seat McCarter Theatre. When Linda Ronstadt's *Heart Like a Wheel* went platinum, she was bumped up to the 1,500-seat Dillon Gymnasium for her double bill with John Prine. But for the Beach Boys, only the 7,000-seat Jadwin Gym would do. Such was their continuing appeal, fully eight years after their last number one hit.

By seven the evening of the Beach Boys' show, the campus was buzzing. As Reef and I walked its full breadth, from Hamilton Hall to Jadwin, we witnessed one dormitory after another emptying before us. And the scene of honor students fleeing their self-imposed captivity outside Firestone Library looked like a jail break. For every uptight, striving, perfect-college-board-scoring student raised to resist the temptations of youthful diversion, it was game on for the Beach Boys.

Reef and I filed into our tenth-row center seats, looked around at the crowd and at the stage, then turned to each other and nodded in approval. "Well, all right!" For some reason, and I would soon find out why, we weren't even high. Was the Reef Man trusting our heads to the complex harmonies of these surfer dudes from Hawthorne, California? Was he trading in his paranoia jones for a pair of baggies and the bushy-bushy blonde epiphanies of "Surfin' U.S.A.?"

Not a chance. Ten minutes before show time, as the Beach Boys' equipment crew checked the microphones and the amplifier connections one last time, Reef handed me a small amber-colored vial with a tiny little spoon on a tiny little chain attached to its top. He told me to put it in my pocket and take it into a men's-room stall. "Use the spoon to snort the white powder up each nostril," he instructed. "If you'd like, you can rub some on your gums."

The B-Side of Paradise

Since I had no idea what this white powder was, and whether it would deliver a "break on through to the other side" high, a spirit-destroying addiction, or instant cardiac arrest, I did exactly what I was told. Following a ribbon of classmates to the men's room, I wondered if they all had small amber-colored vials with tiny spoons in their pockets, too. The answer came soon enough when one by one, they peeled off to the sinks and urinals. While I secured myself a seat in one of the blue stalls with the short doors.

Inside, I found the little spoon easy to use and I snorted one spoonful of the white powder into first my right and then my left nostril, just as Dan advised. Since there were no dosage instructions on the tiny amber vial, I loaded the spoon again. And again. When I felt a slight tightening around my cheekbones and temples, I took that as a sign that this new drug experience might be near liftoff. I tried another spoonful in each nostril and waited for the wind beneath my wings.

Then I remembered what Reef told me about rubbing it on my gums. That delivered a pleasant tingling sensation which I could only describe as like brushing your teeth with peppermint toothpaste and club soda, but without the minty aftertaste.

I was reapplying the white powder to my gums when I heard tuning guitars. The Beach Boys were onstage. There was no time to waste now. I dispensed with the little spoon and put the mouth of the amber-colored vial up to my right and then my left nostril and drained the remainder of its contents. Then I briskly returned to my seat.

There Dan Reefer smiled at me, the smile of the master to the grasshopper. "Everything cool?" he asked. I told him it was and discreetly returned the empty vial. As he furtively replaced it in his jacket pocket, he gave it a glance.

"You did the whole thing?"

"Yeah, why?"

He just said, "Oh." And pocketed the vial. Then we stood up together, as audience members for some reason do at rock concerts, when the Beach Boys kicked into their first song, "Good Vibrations."

In time, I would come to appreciate that Dan Reefer's little amber vial at the Beach Boys' concert had contained a full gram of cocaine before I got my nose around it. And history would one day record my preshow performance as the World's Biggest Bogart. Yet Reef didn't say a word. I was forgiven like a child.

That's one big-hearted cat! I guess it all comes down to how you define remarkable. But in my book, Dan Reefer is an integral part of the great chair that is Princeton and is due a sacred place on the Wiki 650.

Check it out now and see who is there. Carl Icahn? Federal Reserve Bank Chief Jerome Powell? What do you think Chair Powell would say if you snorted up all his coke?

Remarkable Tiger 2:
Andre from the Grove

For some reason, strangers enjoy showing up at my dorm room and rapping their knuckles on my door. I met the second person on my list of remarkable classmates in much the same way as I met Reef. I was in my room listening to the Marshall Tucker Band's "Can't You See" on its third auto-replay when I heard a *tap-tap-tap*. I opened the door, and the stranger gave me one of those "don't worry, the doctor is in" looks and asked, "You want to talk about it?"

The B-Side of Paradise

He was referring to my obsessive playing of "Can't You See" and assumed I was suffering from the same desperate emotional state as the character in the song. If you are not familiar with Marshall Tucker, the song has an upbeat country rock vibe and dark lyrics about heartache and healing.

The chorus is a cowboy's lament about some unspecified behavior of a woman. While the verses are a litany of home-spun remedies for grief culled from Appalachian oral tradition, such as taking a train to nowhere, jumping off the highest mountain, and crawling in a hole in the wall to die.

I laughed and invited him in because that's what you did in college when a stranger knocked on your door and delivered a great line like that. It didn't take long for us to become friends—or for me to recognize he was destined to be a part of the Great Princeton Chair.

I explained that he was misinterpreting things and that I was not pining for some woman like the country boy in the song. But he would have none of it. And he earnestly began probing about my love life. When I told him I had none, he gave me one of those "well, that's our answer isn't it?" looks and tried to assure me my pain would be safe with him.

While I appreciated his concern, and told him so, the truth was I was okay emotionally with where I was relationship-wise, and the only yearning, longing, or burning going on in the room was in the song. He had no reason to worry about me riding a southbound all the way to Georgia until the train runs out of track. I had no plans for the evening. Other than possibly heading up to the Porn Shop (so named for its magazine rack where you could find *Newsweek* or the latest issue of *Juggs*) for a Philadelphia cheesesteak hoagie. Even that wasn't set in stone.

Two Remarkable Tigers

However, in his mind, a man was always sick over a woman. He was either sick over the one he had, sick over the one he just lost, or sick about not having one to be sick over. So, I conceded that I had at times, yearned. And, during periods of yearning, I had sought the solace of blues derivative music. It just wasn't happening that night, though I was thoroughly enjoying Toy Caldwell's tasty guitar licks.

Andre said I was just being stoic, and he knew the signs of heartbreak when he saw them. I said that I knew the signs of when a guy needs a beer and pulled a couple of ice-cold ponies from my minifridge and offered him one. But he declined. In fact, I *never* saw him drink alcohol or touch drugs. But he did ask if I minded his smoking a cigarette.

He reached into his pocket and pulled out a pack of More Silver Menthol Slim 120s which were fully 50 millimeters longer than a regular cigarette. And they were thin and brown—like something Marlene Dietrich might smoke while dressed in a tuxedo and a top hat.

I had not expected, when he asked me if he could have a smoke, to see him pull out something that was so long and thin and brown. I thought it presented a good opportunity for me to lighten things up with a bit of the kind of snarky little comment that was popular between students at the time.

"If I had known you were going to light up one of those I would have said no," I joked. And that's when he called me Big Burls for the first time.

Andre pulled hard on his Silver Menthol Slim 120 and held the smoke in his lungs. Then he blew that mentholated mixture of tar and nicotine out his nostrils with a disbelieving snort. "Look at Big Burls," he said, "dishin' on Andre." And that was great line number two. From then on, it was

Big Burls. He never used my proper name again. Sometimes it was just Burls. Either way, it was the best nickname anyone ever gave me.

Everything changed between us when he lit up that Silver Menthol Slim 120, including the conversation that night which immediately switched to his girl back home in the Grove—the Coconut Grove section of Miami. She was using again. Heroin. He was worried about her and thinking about leaving school to be with her.

I didn't know what to say. Dating a junkie was not a prospect I had ever imagined for myself. And I suspect Tom, Dudsy, and Harry, not to mention Haiku George, Doug, and Charlie would say the same.

Words like, "Gee, I'm sorry to hear that, Andre. That must be very difficult. Is there anything I can do to help?" were forming in my head. Who knows how it might have changed things between us if I had said that… Or how it might have changed things for him…

But I believed at the time, as I do to this day, that it would be best for everyone if I continued dishing him snark. Again, in that faux contentious manner that was common at the time, I suggested he consider the emotional impact his painful stories might be having on me.

"All right, Andre, you come into my room—uninvited I might add—light up that thing, whatever it is, and then you hit me with a story like that. What makes you think somebody like me can handle this?"

Then he went for what I came to believe was the full Coconut Grove smackdown. Something the brothers in the Grove might say to each other when someone lets their macho down. "Burls," he said, "I do believe you would suck a cock."

Two Remarkable Tigers

It being nineteen years before the Seinfeld episode *The Outing*, I was not equipped with its famous comeback line "Not that there's anything wrong with that." Unable to find an appropriate response, I felt my face tighten into one of those involuntary smiles. He smiled back. When there were no further indications that he was asking me for a date—I developed my Coconut Grove smackdown theory. That I stand by to this day.

Somehow my pattern of deflecting the weighty and uncomfortable matters he really wanted to talk about became the ground rules of our friendship. For some reason, this seemed to make him more comfortable coming to me with his problems. Any time he wanted. He may have even been relieved by the way I trivialized his horrible predicament, because he certainly wasn't afraid to bring the matter up.

I heard plenty. And I listened. But I continued to throw him a wall of snark, as I felt he needed, in hopes it might free his mind from the feculence in his life.

I did weigh in once on his situation, however, and I told him he had to stay at school. I advised that he do whatever he could to help his girl back home and let her know that he would. "But don't leave," And let her know that too. I don't know if I gave him the right advice. Maybe it was cold. Maybe it was bourgeois. But that's what I thought he should do. It's what I thought he needed to hear. And that's what I told him.

He once confessed that he had a tough time concentrating on his classes. Some days I would see him walking across campus and he looked like the saddest person I had ever seen. Unimaginable sadness.

Andre would drop by from time to time to smoke some Silver Menthol Slim 120s, talk about his girl, call me Big Burls, and question my sexual orientation. He got to know all my friends to the point that for a while he was one of us, looped into everything we did on campus or off. And we had a lot of good times.

Once when he was down, he knocked on my door and asked me with sad eyes, "Burls, just what am I staying here for?" I invited him in and told him the story of my first visit to campus the summer before my senior year in high school. I told him about my dad and the black squirrels. How he never stopped talking about them. How that's probably why I wound up coming here. And even if that wasn't a very good reason, I was staying because this is the place I chose.

And that's why he should stay, too. Because this was the place he chose. Then he said it again, "Burls, I do believe you would suck a cock."

Andre was a yellow-tag tennis recruit, status inactive just like me. And he carried a green tag, too. But he's more than the tags the Princeton admissions office attached to his application. He is the beating heart of the Wiki 650—for the nickname he gave me, for how he worried about his girl, and because he stayed.

One day, we met up walking across Cannon Green, and he told me that he couldn't hang with me anymore. "The brothers are on my case, Burls. Gotta hang with them for a while." "Andre," I said to him, "I cannot even believe your life."

"Tell me about it."

I asked if I could try one of his Silver Menthol Slim 120s before he left. He reached in his pocket and handed me one. I put it to my lips. He pulled his lighter and lit it for me. I took a drag and held the menthol smoke in my lungs for a bit and then let it out.

"I'll check you, Burls," he said.

Then he walked away and disappeared into his own unfathomable green tag *B-Side*. And that was that.

Lester Lanin
Goes to College

As if I wasn't exploding enough social norms at Princeton, it had all been small-arms fire compared to the day I blew the whole place up. The bombshell news was my bid to Ivy, Princeton's oldest and most prestigious eating club. When word got out that the House of Scribner was dipping its Gucci loafer onto *The B-Side,* the popped collars on Prospect Street grew stiff, swearing as they did that the whole Western world was going to hell in a handbasket.

Imagine, if you can, the scene in the Marx Brothers movie *Duck Soup,* when Gloria Teasdale commanded Freedonia's government ministers to install Rufus T. Firefly as their leader if they ever wanted to see another penny from her. That's the kind of stir my Ivy bid created. For, like Mrs. Teasdale, as Old Fitz wrote in his big-shot debut novel *This Side of Paradise,* the Ivy Club was "detached and breathlessly aristocratic." And, like Firefly, I was equally detached and breathlessly not.

Ivy is one of the eleven eating clubs housed in the grand nineteenth-century mansions that line Princeton's Prospect

The B-Side of Paradise

Street. These privately owned institutions were originally designed to serve the nominal role of providing elevated dining options for students in their junior and senior years, but over time also became a major social center on campus.

Depending on who you talk to, the Prospect Street clubs are either a treasured part of the undergraduate social scene, where valuable friendships are forged for life, or elitist relics of a prewar WASP America. Whether one views these clubs as a source of golden memories waiting to happen or institutionalized microaggressions, most people agree they have grand staircases and handsome billiard rooms.

Princeton's eating clubs have their roots in the Nassau Hall fire of 1855, a blaze that temporarily put the university out of the food business. With its dying embers still aglow, students started grubbing up with friends at local eateries and boarding houses. Their newly formed "dining circles" were temporary and quickly bussed away at graduation, along with the dessert plates from their last meal.

But the tradition was handed down to the next Tiger litter who formed new dining circles. And with that, the roux had been stirred and, in 1879, Arthur Hawley Scribner and friends rented a house, hired a cook and created Ivy.

In a world without fraternities, the Prospect Street clubs soon cornered the campus party market. If you are confused about how an eating club differs from a fraternity, I am, too. However, if you can trust my research (and you shouldn't), it has something to do with the fact that eating clubs are exclusive to Princeton, non-residential, and use real words for names instead of those funny Greek letters that sound like math functions, such as Alpha Delta Pi.

Ninety-five years later, "The Street's" dominant social role on campus was still in full swing. Although club parties were not everyone's favorite Jell-O shot, they were often the most fun you could have on campus without a bag of weed and a Bob Dylan album. In keeping with its tony membership, Ivy Club had the fanciest parties. And its formals with the Lester Lanin Orchestra were always the event of the season.

According to *The New York Times*, Lester Lanin was the undisputed "Bandleader of High Society." From 1927 until his death in 2004, Lester and his orchestra played everywhere and anywhere the rich and powerful gathered. From the White House and Buckingham Palace to the ballrooms of the Vanderbilts and Rockefellers. And the Ivy Club. Many times.

For those of us who need an analogy to understand anything these days, the Lester Lanin Orchestra was to Ivy what the Grateful Dead was to Bill Graham's Fillmore West. Try to imagine the jarring transition as the soundtrack of my life segued from "Uncle John's Band" to the melodies that made the Vanderbilts' toes tap. The whirling dervish dancers, staples in the crowd at Dead concerts, replaced by scores of clicking Balenciaga's fox-trotting in the Ivy Club ballroom. A step that, having two left feet and no formal training, I was ill-prepared to take.

About when the fox-trotters rock-stepped into their Lindy moves (and because there's just so long one could hover over the punch bowl), I would routinely leave the formals and return to my dorm room, where sometime between "'S Wonderful" and "(You'd Be So) Easy to Love," you could find me three pipe cleaners deep into the tight places of my glass bong. There's nothing like a little light housekeeping on a Saturday night. Because a clean bong is a healthy bong.

Over the years, Ivy has filled its membership rolls with Rockefellers, Fords, and Wanamakers. Several generations of the Scribner family tied on the old feed bag in Ivy's elegant, Sheffield silver candelabra-lined dining room. As did Woodrow Wilson, the twenty-eighth President of the United States and champion of such progressive causes as the League of Nations, women's suffrage, and the segregation by race of the federal civil service.

Even the Saudi Arabian diplomat and member of the Saudi royal family, Saud bin Faisal Al Saud (who, as legend has it, loved the creamed chipped beef so much, he once requested thirds), was a proud Ivy member. What inquiring minds want to know, of course, is: If Ivy was the club of Arrow collars and Coolidge dollars, then, why me? Allow me to explain.

The Historic Bicker Dialogs

One night, when the Gentleman's Pipe Club of Hamilton Hall was convened, Harry asked, "So, are we all joining an eating club?" In keeping with my established pattern of being thoroughly in the dark about some of the most manifest things in my life, I said, "What's an eating club?"

Of course, they didn't believe I was serious because…I don't know…the eating clubs are a big thing at Princeton. But they weren't to me. When I revealed that I had never heard of Prospect Street, either, it was time to fire up Old Army. And so, the historic Bicker Dialogs had begun.

As I learned from Harry and Dudsy that night, sophomores with even a hint of social ambition were advised through some Tiger lore I must have missed to attend the fall open houses at one or more of the clubs. The goal was to work one's way into the good graces of a few members who might grease the wheels for them when Bicker season begins.

Lester Lanin Goes to College

Bicker is the eating club's version of a fraternity rush in the same way that Superday at Morgan Stanley is a version of walking into TGI Fridays with your resume and asking to see the manager. Bicker substitutes three days of regimented interviews with club members—that may be intimidating, snark-filled, or fun—for the informal fraternity rush party. Think of it like speed dating, except you're trying to get into the dining room instead of the bedroom.

During that first night of the historic Bicker Dialogs, Tom, Dudsy, and Harry shared their knowledge of Bicker protocols with me. Most of which didn't interest me very much, but I remember them saying something about sport jackets being recommended, because I didn't own one.

After Old Army made several rounds of the smokers' circle, we all pledged to join the same club and began devising our Bicker game plan. We quickly eliminated Ivy. They said it wasn't even worth discussing. Cap and Gown fell next. Too preppy, too pretty, and too polite. Then we tossed Tower Club aside like an old Peter Frampton album. Too much emphasis on extra-curricular activities; clutter we had long since purged from our lives.

"They won't like us very much," Dudsy warned.

"And we won't like them, either," Harry added.

After identifying all the clubs that we wouldn't like, based on who Dudsy and Harry agreed wouldn't like us, we were left with Cottage and Tiger. Harry and Dudsy had already developed a small network at these two mesomorph-friendly clubs generally considered worth opening a vein for— that they were confident Tom, and I could glom onto.

Tom offered a fallback plan in case we couldn't engineer a clean sweep at either. His idea was to target one of the less popular clubs that might go for a package deal. The geographically undesirable Charter Club located at the very end of Prospect Street was the obvious choice.

All anyone knew about Charter was that it held Friday night marathon poker games. And its president, who we only knew by his trade name— the "Cincinnati Kid," was rumored to be a real shark. "We'll button-hole Cincinnati and tell him the Gentleman's Pipe Club of Hamilton Hall is ready to Bicker," Tom said. Sometimes you have to like the way preppies think.

Tom wasn't comfortable with the whole idea of groveling for social acceptance. He was used to other people groveling for his. And he wasn't looking to make friends, either. As far as he was concerned, any facility with a kitchen, media room, and game room where we could take our act on the road would do.

"If we have to, we can always lose a few hands at the table," he said. And with that, it was all for one and one for all. We would take the best offer that came our way. In descending order: Cottage, Tiger, and Charter.

Saud al Faisal's Third Serving of Creamed Chipped Beef

The next day, I went to Harry Ballot, the men's store on Nassau Street that had outfitted the likes of Jimmy Stewart, Bill Bradley, and other fabled alumni. Harry was a master storyteller, with tales of former students, now lions of Wall Street, who so trusted his haberdasher's instincts, that he would send them a half-dozen suits, every season, sight unseen. Before long, I was getting the blue blazer lecture. "Every man's closet should start with the basics," he told me.

But I had my eye on a tasteful blue Harris Tweed fleck

jacket. It reminded me of the one the professor in Prospect Garden wore on my first visit to campus. Coordinated with my faded jeans, a pair of black Bass Weejuns, and an iconic Grateful Dead skull-and-roses T-shirt fashioned after an illustration from a 1913 edition of *Rubaiyat of Omar Khayyam*, I would be dressed for a very successful Bicker. Or so I thought.

Back at the room, Tom, Dudsy, and Harry had called to order an emergency meeting of the historic Bicker Dialogs. They were discussing a stunning takedown of the club scene they read in the *Daily Princetonian* that morning. The clubs, as their history goes, had inspired student protests since the 1920s for their elitist legacies and byzantine Bicker system that left some students without a bid at any club. Scraped from the dinner plate of campus social life, so to speak, and tossed in the trash like the leftovers from Saud Al Faisal's third serving of creamed chipped beef...

In the 1950s, the university pressured the clubs to take the sting out of Bicker. They instituted a "No Hose" policy whereby everyone who bickered would be guaranteed at least one club bid, thus preventing anyone from getting "completely hosed." In 1967, a dozen Ivy members resigned in protest inspiring a Bicker boycott the next year. Eventually, the university created dining alternatives and a new residential college system.

But by 1974, the revolution was over and a "new normal" as the *New York Times* put it in an article that year, had descended on a now "apathetic Princeton." Still, we questioned, "Is this whole club thing totally uncool?" Because if it was, we didn't want to be a part of it.

After looking at all sides of the issue, we agreed the club system *was* totally uncool. But so were the alternatives.

Besides, Harry and Dudsy liked the clubs. Tom could care less. And I already bought my sport jacket. So, it was game on for Street Week.

Street Week

Our first stop was Charter Club where we caught the Cincinnati Kid dealing a game of five-card stud. We approached the table and Tom charmed the silk braces off him. In short order, we exited the club confident that Plan B was in the bag.

Then it was off to Tiger and Cottage, where we met Harry and Dudsy's friends. We were then split up to fight mano a mano for our social lives. And, trust me, the competitive social juices were running like blood in the street. After that, we all had different schedules, so we scattered to fend for ourselves at the remaining clubs.

As Harry predicted, they didn't like my serve or my backhand at Cap and Gown, where I had the women's tennis team captain in visible distress throughout our entire conversation. She was struggling to maintain eye contact while sneaking furtive glances at my *Rubaiyat of Omar Khayyam* T-shirt— hating herself for the discomfort she couldn't conceal and hating me for her self-loathing.

At one point, she was so distraught, I wanted to take her in a big Steppenwolf love embrace and say, "It's okay. You can blackball me. We're not counting on bids from Cap and Gown, anyway." But there was a rule that you had to attend all your Bicker appointments to be guaranteed a "No Hose" bid and I thought it might count as a forfeit, so I kept my mouth shut.

Next, I could feel the chill winds swirling around Tower on the way in and the way out. Interview after interview,

I tried to explain how my main extracurricular activity was quitting all the non-scholastic high-school pursuits I had planned on participating in at Princeton…which I thought, at the least, might be a good conversation starter. I was prepared to make the case that quitting can be character building. But they didn't bite.

Then it was on to Ivy, where I was greeted by what appeared to be a pair of fifty-year-old bankers from the 1920s who insisted they were students and members of the club. I told them they were way too old to be in college and asked to see their student IDs. I think they thought that was funny. There was so much flannel, tortoiseshell, and button-tufted leather in the club I thought I might have been on the set of the History Channel's *The Men Who Built America*.

"My name is Bob, but everybody calls me Jefe."

"My name is also Bob, but you can call me Sherlock. Are you here to Bicker?"

"No, I'm just here to drop off some papers for Mr. Morgan."

"J.P. Morgan," I explained. "He does work here, doesn't he?" Turns out they had a sense of humor, so they invited me into a room with green walls and green leather chairs that they called the Green Room. Because, what else would you call it?

Contrary to popular mythology, no one at my Ivy Bicker sessions called me "Old Sport" or asked me where my family summered. It's possible that others have fielded such off-putting questions. But in my experience, the Ivy crowd is savvier than that. In their world, if they didn't know your bloodlines before you entered the club, then they already knew you were a nobody. So, why bother?

Jefe, Sherlock, and I started off with some light banter. Then they asked several open-ended questions (the kind I used to dread on exams after whizzing through the multiple-choice section), such as "What do you think we do here at Ivy all day." Mergers? Acquisitions?

Then they asked a more hypothetical question—one they claimed was an Ivy standard for situations like mine: "What would you do if you had a million dollars?" Before I could answer, they offered a legendary tale from the dusty old *Book of Ivy* about someone who replied, "I'd change it into nickels and cram it up your ass." Then, by way of instruction, Jefe added, "He got a bid."

"Jefe, Sherlock," I said, shifting in my chair, "I think I'm getting an idea what you do at Ivy all day." They seemed to like that, too. "And although I might like to be part of it, if I had a million dollars, the last thing on my mind would be whose ass to cram it up. However, if I ever felt so inclined, I can assure you I would consider yours first."

For some reason these guys were loving me. And for the duration of Street Week, even I could figure out they were masking and whipping me through Bicker, shielding me from anyone whose votes they couldn't control, and introducing me only to safe members of their caucus. Then they thanked me for coming and said they would be getting back to me. To be honest, I wasn't sure if I should take that as a promise or a threat.

A week later, our bids magically arrived through our mail slots. As expected, we all got bids from Charter, and roundly applauded Tom for his well-conceived and executed plan. To no one's surprise, we got the thumbs down at Tower and Cap and Gown. Then disaster struck. Harry, Dudsy, and I all got bids to Cottage and Tiger. Tom got hosed.

No one could have seen this coming. Tom, the poster child for the Princeton eating clubs' elitist and exclusionary ways, got hosed from every house on the Street except

Charter. It wasn't supposed to work this way. Harry, who knew Tom better than Tom knew himself, asked the obligatory question, "Were you *trying* to rub people the wrong way? Or just not trying very hard to impress?"

As Tom was sheepishly owning up to how his impatience with striving humanity had messed things up for our Gentleman's Pipe Club, there was yet another in what was becoming a long series of consequential knocks on the door in my life: It was Jefe and Sherlock personally delivering my bid to Ivy Club.

Coupled with Tom's industrial-sized hose job, my Ivy bid was a WTF double bill unlike anything the Gentleman's Pipe Club of Hamilton Hall could have imagined. After the Ivy reps left, we sat motionless in our circle of club chairs. There were no words. There was nothing. There was nothing left in the established order that made any sense to us. We were all nihilists now. The *Daily Princetonian* was right. Bicker is a bitch.

Days later, when we finally recovered, we circled around for what would be the final night of the historic Bicker Dialogs to make a game plan for sign-in night. It did not go well. Harry and Dudsy informed us that they were undecided, but it was clear they were backing off our pledge. The fact was they were thrilled with Cottage.

This left me with two untenable options: abandoning Tom to join them or joining Charter with him, with no guarantee he would ever show for a single meal. So emotionally blotto-ed were we, the best we could do was agree to meet up at some unspecified time and some unspecified place on sign-in night. And decide what to do then.

There were still eight weeks left to the semester and Old Army's deployment was far from over. In the days ahead, there would be many more Rolling Rock pony bottles, and Saturday nights watching Murderers' Row.

There's something about sophomore year that is mythical if you do it right. We did it right. We managed to have fun every day without falling down a rabbit hole. But this was the end of the Gentleman's Pipe Club of Hamilton Hall, and we all knew it.

It was a year to remember. The group that lives in you forever. We came together because Tom knew Harry who knew Dudsy who knew me—and we became one. But the eating clubs were breaking up that old gang of ours. After this, we would scatter for the rest of our college days for no good reason—as if sophomore year never happened.

Sign-In Night

It should come as no surprise that we never met anywhere that night. Personally, I didn't make it past Ivy. As I was buttoning the bottom button (and only the bottom button, as Harry Ballot instructed) on my new blue blazer—my second sartorial acquisition since learning of the Princeton eating club phenomenon—there was the fourth consequential knock on my door in my college career.

It was the two Bobs who go by Jefe and Sherlock, there to escort me to Ivy for an early sign-in. "I would be happy to join you," I told them. "But I can't sign in anywhere until I meet up with my roommates." And then, in the reassuring voice of the assassin readying their prey for the kill, they said, "Of course."

When we arrived, Ivy's venerable oak door had barely closed behind us before a vodka martini with a strip of lemon peel was in my hands. For the next three hours, I was never without a full glass. Wherever I went all night, from the famous Green Room to the library, billiards, music, or TV room, if a Smirnoff martini wasn't already waiting for me, it would soon arrive.

Jefe and Sherlock introduced me to all their friends that night. And in an amazing series of coincidences, every one of them had just received news that was worthy of a celebratory toast. And because it is against Ivy party bylaws to turn down a member's toast on sign-in night, as Jefe and Sherlock graciously explained to me, I was obliged to join them for each one.

After running out of fingers to count how many martinis I had had, I met Jefe on the landing of the imperial staircase overlooking the grand foyer below, where Ivy members were assembling for a sign-in ceremony. At the time, I didn't know it would be mine.

"Are you ready?"

And, for the first time that evening, I became aware of the sounds of the Lester Lanin Orchestra. When they got to "You're the Top" from Cole Porter's 1934 hit musical *Anything Goes*, I began my descent. Arm in arm, Jefe and Sherlock guided me down the imperial staircase (the fiery hue and geometric design of its Heriz runners disorienting me in ways the Smirnoff could only imagine) without incident.

There were no creepy candle ceremonies or paddling gauntlets at an Ivy initiation. You just drank a shot of vodka with an oyster at the bottom, everyone sang "Old Nassau," and the deed was done.

One doesn't have to be a Shakespearean scholar to get the "Why then, the world's mine oyster" reference. A metaphor so fitting for this privileged crowd, some might find it offensive. On the other hand, you gotta love their self-aware-ness. Anyway, I was ready for my oyster.

But my oyster wasn't ready for me. Because just to enhance the hundred-year storm of pain I would feel in the morning, when I drained my shot, it got stuck at the bottom. As if the fates were giving me one last chance to reconsider the action I was taking.

Someone poured another shot. I tossed it back and once again the willful bivalve gripped the bottom like it was cling-ing to life itself. For the third time my glass was filled with the same result. Even the oyster knew something dreadfully wrong was taking place. And it was doing its best to prevent it.

Mercifully, on the fifth attempt the piano player dipped his pinky into my glass and released the by-now exhausted little pearl-maker from the bottom. This time, it went down. The pianist played. Everyone sang "Old Nassau." And boom, I was in the front door at Gatsby's, filling my coupe from the champagne tower with the feathered boas and flapper stilt-walkers.

A Low, Miserable Social-Climbing Whore

When I woke up the next morning, there was no way to convince my head it didn't hurt. I tried to remember what it was like before the pain. Before the vodka. Before Ivy. Before I turned out to be a low, miserable social-climbing whore. Alas, one can't fight one's nature. My greatest gift was my greatest curse. I was a chameleon, and no one could insinuate themselves into more places they didn't belong than me.

Lester Lanin Goes to College

Next to Orientation Week, it was the worst "what have I done to myself now?" moment of my life. With scores of dancing Balenciaga's heel-tapping the best-selling *Lester Lanin Goes to College* on my head, I wondered if it was too late to crawl into Cottage Club on my hands and knees and beg for forgiveness. Not that that would matter. I was never long for any organization I joined.

Running through a spectrum of emotions from dread to panic I came to an odd peace with myself that perhaps I had been searching for since failing to find Haiku George, Doug or Charlie my first day on campus. Since I had to eat somewhere, I thought, I might as well dine where I would disrupt the social order the most.

That's what I did best, after all—just ask Old Jenks.

Henceforth, I would owe my allegiance to the feudal lord that was this strange picaresque adventure I was living—and maybe even starting to enjoy. I would walk over hot coals or give myself up to absolute pleasure if it would advance my ill-fated and glorious Ivy League narrative. And I would take notes. If not for this, why was I here?

So, I reached for the comforting wisdom of my mother. Who always used to tell me, whenever life thrust me into uncharted waters, "It's good to get out and see how other people live." Of course, my mother grew up chasing lumps of coal falling from the backs of trucks to keep warm in the winter—so what did she know?

I'm not sure when the two Bobs who go by Jefe and Sherlock found me under the button-tufted leather couch in the Green Room. But somehow, after they lifted that verdant chesterfield off me, they transported me to PJ's Pancake House where they fed me coffee and buckwheat pancakes with sugary syrup and salty bacon, much like they had plied me with potato spirits the night before. They said everything was going to be fine. "There are some really great guys in the club." They told me they were trying to change the club's image.

Which brings us back to Groucho Marx, who famously said, "I don't want to belong to any club that would accept me as a member." But what would Groucho say about joining a club that would only have you as a member to shield itself from criticism that it doesn't have any members like you?

Destined to play the Nick Carraway role, I sharpened my pencil and reminded myself (lest I write too critically of my new Ivy friends) of his father's advice in *The Great Gatsby*: "… remember that all the people in this world haven't had the advantages that [I've] had."

"Are we cool?" Jefe asked.

"Yeah. We're cool."

The Butler's Guide
to Clothes Care

There's a scene in *This Side of Paradise* where Amory Blaine and his friend Rahill lie about their St. Regis dormitory room blowing smoke rings and imagining misfortune on their least favorite classmates. Whom amongst them are destined for success? And who is more likely to wind up working in their father's painting business, marrying, and having four bonehead kids?

All St. Regis men, Amory postulated, except for Philosophers like himself and Rahill, fall into one of two categories from which their futures may be foretold: the slicker or the big man.

The Slicker, according to Amory, is easy to recognize by the "badges of their slicker hood." Namely, slicked back hair and tortoiseshell glasses. They dress well, but act like they don't care about clothes, engage only in activities where they are sure to succeed, and have a keen sense of social norms.

The Big Man acts from a sense of duty, is a careless dresser, is "inclined to stupidity" and "unconscious of social values," and has a "problematic future." I think we all know which category you can find your trusted narrator.

Amory's foresight was not limited to how well he could see me coming. His paradigm worked equally well to describe the Ivy Club dining room, fifty years later. Specifically, the social divide between its two long tables that together could accommodate the entire sixty-member club.

The table on the left was the Slickers' table. Picture Whit Stillman's *Metropolitan*. Here you would find scions of great wealth whose forebears amassed their fortunes from penning prize-winning asset-pricing models, manufacturing those cute little clown cars they drive in Europe, and making soap. Lots of soap. All kinds of soap.

Big Men were more of an afterthought at Ivy. In fact, there were only two. Me and the Pistol, who you will hear more about in a future chapter. So, I had to sit at the Philosophers' table. Picture Peter Weir's *Dead Poet's Society*.

Despite Ivy's parsimonious embrace of the Big Man, or perhaps because of it, one wasn't granted such exalted status just for being socially backward and destined to a future of mediocrity. You had to earn the stripes on your Big Man Ivy tie through acts of duty and honor and good works on behalf of the club.

This is a story about how I did just that, with such *B-Sided* brio that I received formal recognition from the Slickers themselves. A moment that marked a turnaround in my Tiger career and put me back on track for accomplishments outside the classroom that would result in my receiving three "major university awards."

Gentleman Jack Bourbon

I earned my first Big Man stripe in the service of one Gentleman Jack Bourbon. A pre-med and consummate Philosopher, Gentleman Jack would have been welcomed at the Slickers' table, hailing, as he did, from a wealthy family of Kentucky distillers.

But Bourbon was a master of the psychic mind-fuck. He preferred the company of the Philosophers, especially the god-fearing types, who were provincial in the ways of deviant thought and action to which he was drawn. It provided him with endless amusement to blow their minds with outlandishly modern ideas— using many of the same rhetorical devices bandied about at the Whig-Cliosophic Society meetings that were the keynote in many a Philosopher's week.

The Slickers, cosmopolitan at times to a fault, would have had scant time for that. Leaving Jack, no other recourse than to become a traitor to his class—a man of *The B-Side*, not because he was born into it but because he chose it.

Bourbon was a master at using his Southern drawl to make the most mundane question sound as nuanced and complex as the best top-shelf whiskey. "So, how do you like Ivy so far?" he asked, his words pouring out with strong notes of vanilla, oak char, and cinnamon.

I could tell his question was meant in the ontological sense. What Jack Bourbon was really asking was, "Does your brain still hurt or are you getting used to this place?" So, naturally I gave him the old, "What's not to like? The meat is lean. The rice, light and fluffy." And with that, we were friends.

Bourbon never hesitated to fill an adjacent seat at dinner. And I always reciprocated when there was an empty chair on his flank. One day our paths crossed on the way to the club.

He invited me to join him for dinner, but I had to make a stop first. "Come with me. I'll introduce you to my friend Vonn."

When we arrived, Vonn was draped across his bed like the reclining David that Michelangelo never got around to sculpting. Sporting only a pair of Jockey briefs and a Miller High Life and listening to the Allman Brothers' *At Fillmore East.*

A slave to self-regimentation, Vonn filled his day with electrical engineering classes in the day and a study group at night. His afternoons were set aside for free-weight workouts at Dillon Gym followed by two hours of downtime for muscle recovery and rehydration. A shower, a beer, and two sides of an LP played through his McIntosh power amp and his Acoustic Research speakers was a ritual he always performed in his skivvies.

Bourbon was too mannerly to comment on Vonn's sensuality, but he made a mental note of it. When he discovered the reason for my visit, to return a pack of Zig-Zag papers, he revealed that he was yet another charismatic cannabis entrepreneur Princeton admissions had the good sense to invite into the university community. Promotionally minded as one must be in his line of work, he offered us a complimentary stick of primo Jamaican. "Well," Vonn said, "I hope to see more of you, then."

"I hope to see more of you, too," Bourbon replied.

Waiting for the light to change on the corner of Washington Road and Prospect Street, I entered into a gentleman's agreement with Bourbon that would set me on my path to achieving Big Man status in the club. "*Alfred,*" he said as if pouring a glass of Woodford Reserve Double Oaked Bourbon, "can you do me a favor?"

He continued, coyly, "Can you take me back to Vonn's sometime so I can watch him recline in his tighty-whities?"

And then with hints of sweet oak and vanilla on the nose, leading to a big honey and caramel, creamy finish, "I was so taken with his lemony cupcake pecs, I didn't have a chance to check out his package."

Duty-bound as I was to a fellow Ivy member, I took him to Vonn's the next day. Vonn was clamping the roach from Bourbon's complimentary slim Jamaican with the hemostatic forceps he used as a clip. This time, he was wearing a pair of black BVDs, and I thought the distiller's boy was going to faint. "You remember Jack Bourbon," I said. "Jack, your weed is exquisite. I'm really enjoying this." "I'm enjoying this, too," Bourbon said.

Vonn asked Gentleman Jack if he would like to listen to the Grateful Dead. "Well, maybe if you have something trippy."

"Would *Dark Star* do?"

"That would be lovely."

And there we sat, Vonn smoking his roach through his hemostatic forceps while I read the album cover and Bourbon sat contentedly casting furtive glances at Vonn's junk.

After that, we made it a regular Friday afternoon event. Vonn soon ran out of trippy jam-band music, so Bourbon started bringing over his acid jazz records. He started us off with *Space Is the Place* from Sun Ra and His Intergalactic Solar Arkestra. We moved on in subsequent weeks to Rusty Bryant, Sonny Stitt, and Boogaloo Joe Jones—all legends of the genre.

Later at dinner, Bourbon would wax poetic about Vonn's sculpted body. He was kind enough to spare me the intimate parts. But I remember he liked to compare Vonn's buff arms and chest with biscuits and gravy, cornbread muffins, and other traditional Southern comfort foods.

The B-Side of Paradise

Meanwhile, Vonn and I enjoyed the opportunity to expand our musical horizons and smoke Bourbon's weed. It was a regular mutual admiration society. "He's always welcome," Vonn would say whenever the topic came up. Bourbon, without getting too graphic, was equally effusive about Vonn.

It all came crashing down one morning when my good friend, named after the American corn whiskey his family distilled, made the front page of the *Daily Princetonian*. They called it the biggest campus drug bust in university history. The article went on to detail the treasure trove of evidence the town police found in his room, including ten uncashed checks each in the amount of $30, the going rate for an ounce of weed at the time. One of the checks, inconveniently as these things go, bore my signature.

Envisioning a wider dragnet in the days ahead, I returned to my room and dropped to my knees to pick sticks and seeds from the 9' x 12' area rug on my floor. Everywhere I turned, there was evidence against me. Realizing I needed better technology, I went to Urken Supply Co. on Witherspoon Street and the man with the True Value logo on his chest sold me a Eureka portable vacuum for a deeper clean.

It was no use. Gold, red, and green flakes from some of the world's finest cannabis strains were inextricably woven into the rug fibers. Eventually, I just rolled it up and threw it in a dumpster behind Edwards Hall.

When Bourbon finally returned to the club, he quietly filled the open seat next to me. "What's for lunch?" he asked with his always provocative 90-proof delivery. And just like that, things were back to normal. Though we never spoke of the bust, and as he was bogged down with legal matters, our Friday afternoon Acid Jazz sessions were over.

Nevertheless, my friendship with him did not go unnoticed. Because everybody in the club liked Bourbon (the philosopher *and* the distilled spirit), I received my first gold stripe on my green silk Ivy tie. I collected my second just by being a bad backgammon player, a good liar, and having an Italian heritage.

Power to the Imagination Gio

Most nights before dinner at Ivy there was a backgammon game going on outside the Green Room, often drawing a hushed crowd of spectators around the green button-tufted leather couch and club chairs. Many a carefully executed backgame was played at that table, players silently eying every blot and setting their blockade strategies.

But Gio and I didn't care for blockades. We played our own brand of full-throttle Indy 500–speed backgammon. That amounted to nothing more than one big post-adolescent blot-hitting contest. The faster you could send your opponent's stones to the bar, the better.

Our daredevil moves regularly drew gasps from the buttoned-up crowd. Eventually we would offend some backgammon purist beyond the point of restraint and sounds of indignation would fill the air: a throat-clearing full-two-syllable "ahem."

Then came the breathy whispers, "Hmm, unorthodox move." Gio would throw his hands in the air to protest the sclerotic thinking that surrounded him. "Power to the imagination, my friend!" he would trumpet, chastising the offending mossback.

Of course, there was no greater testament to the power of the imagination than my friendship with Gio at the backgammon board—he in his couture Armani slacks and starched shirts with French cuffs (folded neatly two turns up his arm); me in my untucked flannel top and Lee Rider cords generously salted with washing machine lint. He, a scion of one of Italy's richest families; me, the Flying Christmas Cannoli kid.

Gio would have made an odd pair with anyone. Dripping with grace and beauty and old-world charm, even the courtliest American Slicker was rough around the edges compared to him. Yet we were best buds at the backgammon table and the source of much head-scratching from those who felt at once spurned and more worthy of Gio's attention than me.

Jefe and Sherlock were well-aware of the passion that Gio and I shared for bad backgammon. And on this slim reed of familiarity was I called to duty when international intrigue struck again—this time in Prospect Street's Ivy Club. "You want me to do what?" I asked.

"We want you to get on the phone with Gio's mom and talk her down off the ledge."

Gio, it seemed, had made the mistake of sounding his "power to the imagination" slogan on his last call home to Milan. The rallying cry of the anarcho-Marxist student protests at the Sorbonne in 1968. Student protests that were joined by ten million workers, resulting in the occupation of 122 factories and the declaration of a general strike that crippled the French economy and nearly brought down the government.

Anyway, it got Gio's mom's imagination going, too. And now, fearing he might be in direct contact with elite members of the movement and in danger of being abducted, or that he might join the underground on his own volition, she wanted to pull him out of school and bring him home.

"You do understand I don't know *anything* about Gio?"

"Nobody does. Just say you're his friend. Everything's great," Jefe instructed. "And whatever you do, don't mention 'power to the imagination.'"

Jefe took me to an office on the club's second floor where Sherlock already had Milan on the line. I heard him say, *"Ecco l'amico di Gio. Buona gironata."* Then he stuck the phone to my ear and whispered, "Good luck."

If you were a fly on the wall, you'd hear me living up to the European perception that all Americans are "idiots" when I greeted Gio's mom by saying, "Hello. *Bone jorno!* Do you speak English? Oh, good." And then there was nothing left for me to do but start lying through my teeth. "I'm Gio's friend.... Yes, a good friend.... A *very* good friend.... We play back-gammon. Everybody cheers. Gio is such a good player."

Even though Gio's mother spoke fluent English, I was talking unnaturally loud and slow, as Americans often do with people who don't share our language. In hopes it will help them translate unintelligible sounds into words and concepts they can understand.

"Everybody loves Gio."

She told me she was worried and asked if I had ever heard him say "power to the imagination?"

"No! Nothing. Nothing like that. Never."

There was a long pause. I tried to wait her out, but she was too good. "Well, maybe once. But he was joking. He said, 'the French are crazy, and their wine is overrated.'" Then she let it all out. "I'm sick. Sick over everything. I don't want to live."

Even from 4,000 miles away, I could follow the flight of the cannoli on the other end of the line. Their hard shells crashing into the Titian's and Giotto's hanging on villa walls. Creamy mascarpone filling dripping from the Murano-glass chandeliers. *Splat* onto the marble floors below. I knew I had to do something to change the subject.

"I'm Italian, you know?"

"Ah, Italiano?"

"Yes, *very* Italiano." It was a stroke of genius. "Gio is, too."

She asked, "Where are your parents from?" I didn't think she meant Queens, so I told her Rome. My father's parents were in fact from Rome—and Naples, although my mother's parents were from Stjørdalshalsen and Považská Bystrica. But I didn't think I needed to get into that.

"I have so much to ask you," she said. "Have you ever been to Italy?"

"Yes." I had.

"When?"

"Last summer."

"Where?"

"Rome. And Florence."

"The food *was* good."

"Yes, I saw the Colosseum…. Of course, I went to the Vatican…. No. I think the Pope was out of town."

"I threw *three* coins in Trevi Fountain… Well, that's personal."

"Did you know I have seen every one of Fellini's films? Even *The Nights of Cabiria*."

Then she invited me to Lago di Como where they had a summer villa, told me how happy she was that Gio had such a good friend, and said she hoped to see us play backgammon soon.

"Great job!" Jefe said. Sherlock slapped me an attaboy. And that was how I earned my second Big Man stripe at Ivy Club.

The Night of the Strong, Confident Woman

Walking down Prospect Street one day, I heard a voice call out, "Hey, big fella!" It was a friend from the Henry Hall Ladies Who Lunch Club on her way to Cap and Gown.

"When are you going to take me to dinner at Ivy?" she asked.

"What a great idea!"

"Wouldn't it be?"

"Yes, I will definitely take you to Ivy."

"I hear the Ivy boys get their panties in a twist when somebody brings a lady friend to dinner."

"Like you wouldn't believe," I said.

"Won't *you* be the talk of the club."

"Why didn't I think of this?"

"Because you're just a big dumb galoot."

Everybody knew.

The Gentleman's Pipe Club of Hamilton Hall shared many dinners with the Henry Hall Ladies Who Lunch at Holder Commons the previous year. I'm not sure who knew whom to bring us together for the first time. But once we met, we flocked together like birds of a feather, only to scatter in flight at the end of sophomore year. Another Bicker casualty.

Although "strong, confident woman" was not the mind-numbing refrain in the empowerment chorus of American life that it is today; to reflect current practice, we will call this dear old friend of mine, the SCW. Seeing that she was captain of the swim team. All-Ivy in the Freestyle. Triangle Club lead. Winner of the Francis Biddle Sophomore Prize for Best Essay in American Literature. And sassy, to boot.

The B-Side of Paradise

On the Night of the Strong, Confident Woman, I went with the blue-fleck Harris tweed and a pair of lightly linted brown corduroys. She wore nothing special. A breezy fit-and-flare dress, cotton scarf, and slouchy fabric shoulder bag. Everything about us sent the message, "We've done this before." Even though we hadn't.

Readers unfamiliar with the way owls can turn their heads 270 degrees should check out Season 33, Episode 9 of PBS' *Nature: Owl Power*. If you are back from your TV now, what you just saw was how the heads spun at the Slickers' table when the SCW entered the dining hall that night. If you can't find this *Nature* episode, just think of Linda Blair in *The Exorcist*—you know the scene.

The real head-turner, however, was not that the SCW was there, but that she was there with *me*. Whether the Slickers considered our pairing an unnatural event that inflamed the viscera and had to be witnessed in horror up close, or a great social wrong that had to be righted, they charged our table like we were an evolutionary threat to their herd.

One by one, Slickers who had never seen the world from the Philosophers' side of the club signaled the start of red deer rutting season with a deep stag bellow. Then parallel-walked over and locked horns in competition to impress the SCW.

"I hope you enjoy your stay at Ivy."

"Thank you." Then, clutching my hand and batting a "you don't stand a chance eye," she said, "I already am." One by one, and much to the amusement of everyone at the Philosophers' table, she dispensed with them in her always inspirational SCW way and sent them parallel-walking back to their table—locked horns and all.

"Well, that's a first," said my Rhodes Scholarship obsessed Philosopher friend who I will call Cecil, referring to the Slickers' presence on our side of the dining room.

"Allow me to welcome you to Ivy. My name is Cole Digby. My father strip-mined the state of West Virginia."

"*Enchanté.* I think?"

Even Pistol, who you will hear more from in a future chapter, was impressed. "You two are good. Did you rehearse this?"

"A small group of us are taking dessert in the billiard room. We need a pair to play a round robin, and we'd like to invite the two of you to join us. If you don't have any plans."

"Oh, we have plans," she said in a resounding SCW brush-off that would have had the McCarter Theatre crowd on its feet—and that sent the cocksure slicker slinking back to his seat.

"They're not *good*," Gentleman Jack Bourbon corrected "They're *evil*."

"I think I'm going to be ill," said the SCW.

Then the rave reviews came flooding in. Philosophers and even students of faith from up and down the Philosophers' table leaned in to express their appreciation. Some of the more memorable testimonials we received that evening were, "Thank you. *So* much!" "Most fun I've had in ages." And even a "God bless you. May your souls rest in eternal peace." Everybody was happy to see the Slickers grovel at the Philosophers' table.

Then, the SCW reached her hand out to me. "Take it."

"Excuse me?"

"*Take my hand.*"

"Okay." I reached out and, fighting back those unworthy feelings, wrapped my meaty paw around her delicate leading-lady fingers.

"Look into my eyes," she insisted in her nothing less than extraordinary SCW way.

"Okay."

"Say something."

"Like what?"

"Tell me how happy you are that I could join you."

"Okay."

"And how you've been thinking about this moment for a long time."

"Bourbon was right. You *are* evil!"

"That will do."

And no one bothered us much after that.

Meanwhile, we had a good time drinking the three bottles of wine the sommelier brought us. (Yes, Ivy has a sommelier.) And we both agreed that the food, whatever it was, was very good. On the way out of the dining hall, she leaned in close and stage-whispered, "Whatever you do, *don't* take me on a tour of the club."

"Why?"

"Just get my coat."

After I helped her slip it on, the SCW further instructed, "Put your arm around me. And walk me out." Outside, the cold night air smacked us silly. We threw our heads back in laughter like they do at the end of a Triangle Club first act. "Priceless," she said.

"Everyone thought it was a *real* date."

"It *is* a real date."

"It is?"

Why was I always the last to know?

Somehow, we made it back to my room where we immediately fell backward onto my bed. Once again, she leaned in. "Close your eyes." That was her first mistake of the night. Then I made my first mistake. I closed them. As soon as my lashes met, the room started spinning.

Not to get too into the porcelain on this, but, yes, I worshipped the great white god American Standard on my hands and knees that night. When I returned to the bedroom, the SCW was standing there, looking as strong and confident as ever. Troupers as we both were, albeit in different ways, our eyes met again. And in keeping with our otherwise brilliantly choreographed evening, said, as if on cue, "Rain check?"

The next morning, I took myself to PJ's Pancake House for copious amounts of coffee, buckwheat pancakes, sugary syrup, and salty bacon. "How do you come back from a night like that?" was the topic of conversation I was having with myself. Alas, "there are no second acts in American lives," Old Fitz famously said. And there would be no second act for the Night of the Strong, Confident Woman.

A Sign of Respect

Days later, at the annual holiday awards dinner, I heard my name called out for special club recognition. "Al D'Alessandro, please come to the dais to accept Ivy Club's inaugural Lint on the Pants Award." Then they presented me with a genuine English horn lint brush and a gold-embossed copy of *The Butler's Guide to Clothes Care, Managing the Table, Running the Home & Other Graces.*

Some people have suggested this was more of a putdown than the first of a series of "Major University Awards" I would claim in my time ahead. And more than a few have pointed out that had I merely taken the time to clean the lint trap in the Edwards Hall washing machine, they wouldn't have had reason to recognize me at all.

Those people don't understand Ivy Club. You see, I had

performed dutifully on behalf of Gentleman Jack Bourbon and Gio. On the Night of the Strong, Confident Woman, I brought honor and prestige to the entire club. Not to mention unparalleled joy to the Philosophers' table. One way or another, I was a player now. A Big Man, in all his bonehead glory. The Slickers had to acknowledge that as their code demanded. The fact they did so in condescending fashion was a sign of respect.

The B-Side Picks
the Princeton G.O.A.T.

In 2008, the *Princeton Alumni Weekly* assembled a team of tenured professors to choose Princeton's 25 greatest alumni of all time. They quickly discovered that if they stripped out all the historically significant Tigers whose curricula vitae were aberrant to current "Princeton values," and abhorrent to them personally, they would be left with a paltry few. Faced with either career suicide or publishing a threadbare list, they instead chose Princeton's 25 most *influential* alumni instead.

This opened a spot at #25 for them to include the impressive résumé hog and some would say all-too influential Donald Rumsfeld. The Princeton wrestling champion, who was a four-term U.S. congressman, held three different cabinet-level positions, was also CEO of two Fortune 500 companies, and the architect of the iconic made-for-TV United States invasion of Iraq. Without making it seem like they *approved* of him.

But we have our own values on the B-Side. And we're not afraid to pick a G.O.A.T. Or to offend a few people along the way. That said, to forestall the kind of time-consuming research it has been my life's work to avoid, I started with the *Princeton Alumni Weekly (PAW)* list to see if I could come up with a quick G.O.A.T.

The first person on *PAW's* 25 Most *Influential* Princetonians list was America's fourth president, James Madison. Also known as the Father of the Constitution, Madison is not only Princeton's most influential alumnus, but few Americans have made as significant an impact on our nation's history and its institutions.

Not to go all wobbly on *The B-Side* so soon, but Madison has that thorny issue of being a "slaver." So, I said, "Madison who?" Then moved on to the DEI-challenged and third-ranked Woodrow Wilson. In similar fashion, and in no small part due to the way he was buried like a Joe Pesci hit in the desert when Princeton removed his name from their school of Public and International Affairs, I couldn't remember his name, either.

We may make our own rules on *The B-Side*, but we're not stupid. Things have changed a lot for dead white men since 2008.

That left Alan Turing, the great English mathematician and computer scientist; the political philosopher John Rawls; and physicist John Bardeen from *PAW's* top five. I already mentioned Turing and Rawls in a previous chapter, so I moved on to Bardeen at #5 rather than rehash familiar territory and bore the reader.

Bardeen, I discovered, is the only person to win a Nobel Prize in Physics twice. That sounded impressive to me, and I figured I wouldn't get too roughed up if I chose someone with his credentials, so I made a note of Bardeen and moved on. After #5, however, there just seemed to be something wrong with each person on the list.

The B-Side Picks the Princeton G.O.A.T.

For instance, George Kennan, the great scholar and diplomat who the *PAW* professors ranked #6. Kennan was the guy moving all the big chess pieces in the late 1940s, like the Marshall Plan and the Truman Doctrine that helped rebuild postwar Europe and contain the Soviet Union during the Cold War. Hailed by many as America's greatest twentieth-century diplomat, few Tigers have roared so loud. For a time, at least.

Because Kennan trashed his own legacy like a Pete Townshend guitar when he started opposing everything, or, should I say, the only things that an otherwise divided Washington establishment could agree upon. Such as the Vietnam War, the Iraq War, and NATO expansion. Of course, I was tempted to give it to him precisely for that. But with the drums of war beating again, I dropped the mic on Kennan.

Being a man of letters like Old Fitz, and because this whole exercise was proving to be more work and considerably more dangerous than I had imagined, I thought about giving the G.O.A.T. to the literary master who *PAW* picked for #8, thereby aborting the mission before I got permanently suspended from my social media accounts. But considering the way *The B-Side* is riffing off his book, I decided that might be too incestuous. And honoring Old Fitz would be best left to someone not already shamelessly trading off his good name.

Finally, when I never even heard of numbers #11–#13, I began to lose interest in the *PAW* list. Although I did make a second note to revisit Richard Feynman, another Nobel laureate in Physics at #14.

Then I ditched *PAW* and returned to my trusty Wiki 650, where I found its more expansive universe of remarkable Tigers offered some great possibilities that, frankly, the Princeton professors may not have had the imagination to consider.

The B-Side of Paradise

Such as Juan Marichal, the "Dominican Dandy" who was one of my boyhood idols. A Hall of Famer and nine-time All Star, Marichal bested Warren Spahn 1–0, in a 16-inning game, known to baseball cognoscenti as the Greatest Game Ever Pitched. He was exactly the kind of great Tiger that you would expect a bunch of academic hacks to overlook. Subject to a quick check to confirm his Princeton bona fides, I was ready to name him my G.O.A.T.

Imagine my embarrassment when I discovered that the Juan Marichal who degreed at Princeton was *not* the San Francisco Giant pitcher known for his high leg kick. But a Spanish-Canarian historian. I can assure you my work would have been done if this 1949 Princeton Ph.D. in modern languages and literature had a sharper break on his curveball.

Soon after the "Dominican Dandy" fiasco, I received an invitation to one of the '76 *Together Apart Zoom* meetings my Tiger class hosted during the COVID pandemic. For each session, the class officers invited prominent classmates to discuss—whatever, I never read them that carefully. At this upcoming meeting Eric Schmidt, who co-founded Google with Larry Page and Sergey Brin, was going to speak. In 2007, *PC World* named the trio #1 on their 50 Most Important People on the Web list.

I liked Eric as my pick because I could not have written this book without him. Seeing that I am already on my 10,000th visit to Thesaurus.com. That, according to psychology professor Anders Ericsson's 10,000-Hour Rule, popularized in Malcolm Gladwell's *Outliers*, would make me as good at searching up synonyms on the internet as the Beatles were at making music. Or at least as good as they were when they left Hamburg in 1962.

The B-Side Picks the Princeton G.O.A.T.

But Eric didn't make the *PAW* committee's Top 25, and Jeff Bezos did. I couldn't give it to Schmidt when Bezos was out there. However, I had a bone to pick with Bezos. At the expense of seeming ungrateful, I will thank him here for helping me out of a tight spot when I found some drop-ceiling tiles on Amazon that were out of stock at Lowe's and Home Depot. But I wouldn't trade that convenience for the splendid hours I've missed thumbing the book and CD racks at Borders. Thanks for ruining everything, Jeff.

That's when I decided to return to my Nobel Prize winners in Physics. John Bardeen and Richard Feynman. Bardeen had the edge, coming in at #5 on the *PAW* list and for winning the Nobel twice: once for the invention of the transistor that paved the way for every electronic device we use today and ushered in the Information Age, the second for the BCS (Bardeen-Cooper-Schrieffer) theory on "conventional" superconductivity. Which has something to do with MRI machines—and levitating trains. Seriously. Anyway, few STEM careers have been as influential as his.

Unfortunately, I soon discovered that Bardeen has a name recognition problem. Against all odds, John was the subject of a 2019 article in *Science Focus* titled, "The Greatest Physicist You (Probably) Never Heard Of." Despite being memorialized in an American Scientists postage stamp series along with Linus Pauling and Edwin Hubble just ten years earlier. Both of whom managed to become famous in a manner that seems to have escaped Bardeen. I didn't have the time or the inclination to find out what Bardeen was hiding in his closet, and I needed a stronger hook for this book, so, I moved on to Feynman.

I got a good feeling about Feynman right away. And not just because he received prominent mention in Ranker.

com's "Celebrities Reveal What They Hallucinated While Tripping." Where he reported "powerful out of body experiences" while high on ketamine in an isolation tank. As well as seeing the back of his own head. Something I suspect no one on *PAW*'s Top 25 list could match. With, of course, the possible exception of Donald Rumsfeld. Additionally, Feynman is joined on Ranker's list by the likes of Jack Nicholson, Chelsea Handler, Rebel Wilson, and Miley Cyrus. Which didn't exactly hurt his chances.

Feynman's credentials, I soon learned, are manifold. He won the Nobel Prize for his work in quantum electrodynamics, assisted in the development of the atomic bomb, and was voted #7 in *Physics World*'s 1999 survey of the greatest physicists of all time. A list that includes Sir Isaac Newton, Albert Einstein, and Galileo Galilei. G.O.A.T. heaven for physicists.

He was also a pop culture rock star, the subject of the documentary *The Pleasure of Finding Things Out*, as well as feature films such as the 1996 biographical drama *Infinity* starring Matthew Broderick. And the 2013 TV movie *The Challenger* about his investigation into the tragic 73-second flight of the Space Shuttle.

Feynman racked up additional points when I discovered he had a modest 125 IQ. Who doesn't love a highly revered smart guy who isn't even that smart? What's more, he is widely acclaimed for his ability to discuss science in a way regular people can understand, such as his famous quote, "Physics is to mathematics what sex is to masturbation." Which explained my son Beckett's interest in vectors and projectiles.

But it wasn't until I read his national bestselling book, *Surely You're Joking, Mr. Feynman!* that I started to get serious about naming him my G.O.A.T. Especially the part where he described how his undergraduate MIT friends all predicted that the socially challenged Feynman would be a total misfit at Princeton.

In fact, Feynman did famously commit an unconscionable faux pas in Tiger Town when he requested both milk *and* lemon at his first afternoon tea with the dean of the graduate school. Prompting the dean's wife to exclaim, "Surely you're joking, Mr. Feynman." A line he cleverly repurposed for the title of his book.

Other red flags were present in Feynman's early career. Namely, his penchant for getting distracted with pop science. Such as his experiments in hypnosis, mind reading, and picking the locks to the desks of the army brass at Los Alamos—just to embarrass them and demonstrate that their atomic secrets were not as well guarded as they might have thought.

Perhaps the greatest example of Feynman's at times puerile quest for knowledge was his human bloodhound research. Determined to see if humans' sense of smell could rival the bloodhound, Feynman had his wife handle a book on their bookshelf and replace it where she found it. He then proceeded to sniff all the books and was able to pick the one she had touched.

He followed up with a similar trial using Coke bottles in his refrigerator that was also successful. However, when Feynman dropped to his knees to see if he could pick up the scent of his own footprints in the carpet, as his dog did routinely, he failed. Only then did he concede that bloodhounds can discern scents better than humans can. Something no one ever disputed.

The Japanese navy straightened him out when they attacked Pearl Harbor on December 7, 1941. And he landed a sweet summer gig doing ballistics work for the army. Meanwhile, his research at Princeton also impressed to the extent that by the age of twenty-three, he was already recognized as one of the greatest theoretical physicists on earth. Before he completed his Princeton thesis, he was recruited to work on the Manhattan Project at the Los Alamos Laboratory in New Mexico.

Feynman led the Los Alamos team charged with doing the theoretical work on separating uranium isotopes, while another group of lab scientists in a plant in Oak Ridge, Tennessee, was responsible for physically separating the uranium. A little-known fact about the Oak Ridge operations was that America's military brass—secretive at times to a fault—never told the lab scientists they were making a bomb. They had no idea the purified uranium they were handling was highly explosive. Until Feynman was sent to inspect the plant.

He found that if it wasn't completely redesigned, along with the way the lab scientists stored and handled the uranium, the Oak Ridge Boys would never grow up to write "Elvira" and make it to the Country Music Hall of Fame. Feynman convinced the army brass that he had to let the plant scientists know they were handling materials for the most lethal bomb the world has ever known if they expected him to make the dramatic changes required at the plant. Eventually they agreed.

The story had a happy ending, at least for everyone outside the Hiroshima and Nagasaki metropolitan areas, when the United States detonated two atomic bombs in August 1945. Which ended the war in the Pacific and paved the way for a mutually beneficial alliance between Japan and America—one that resulted in the outsourcing of American radio, television, and washing machine manufacturing to Japan. And the proliferation of trendy sushi restaurants in American cities and inner-ring suburbs in the 1980s.

After the war, Feynman became a professor at Cornell University. Burdened by the weight of his genius and the expectations of others, he got burned out and his research faltered. That's when the man who would one day write a second autobiography titled *What Do You Care What Other People Think?* decided it was time to get back to doing what he did best. Which was to get on his hands and knees and sniff the carpet.

Sitting in the cafeteria one day, a student was spinning a plate with the red Cornell medallion in the middle and Feynman noticed that the medallion was spinning faster than the rest of the plate. A worthy scientific inquiry for the young impetuous Feynman, he thought, and one that might take his mind off his researcher's block. Running through some calculations revealed that the medallion spun twice as fast as the rest of the plate. But he didn't know why.

He tried to involve other physics professors in his further inspection, but they all thought it was frivolous and didn't want to play his game. As history would have it, that line of study led to his Nobel Prize–winning research in quantum electrodynamics.

What exactly is quantum electrodynamics? Who knows? Who cares? Honestly, he had me with the hallucinations.

That's how you pick a G.O.A.T. on the B-Side of Paradise.

The Pistol:
My G.O.A.T. Classmate

What if I used the Feynman methodology to pick a second G.O.A.T? My Greatest Tiger Classmate. This person would have to exhibit the same charming indifference to others and youthful enthusiasm for self-entertainment that shot Feynman up the charts and to the top of my Greatest of All Time Princeton Alumni list.

Proceeding from this carefully constructed mandate leaves me with only one choice: the Pistol. The other Big Man in Ivy Club. Pistol and Feynman were soulmates, except for all the STEM stuff. Their lives were never-ending quests for amusement, and they didn't give a boyish hoot what other people thought about them.

Pistol had three great dreams he hoped to pursue at Princeton. They involved Pistol Pete Maravich, the Hall of Fame basketball player; Bruce Catton, the Pulitzer Prize–winning American Civil War historian; and the British rock and pop band, the Hollies. Each was shattered by the Princeton Way. Except for his Hollies fantasy that I crushed.

The Pistol: My G.O.A.T. Classmate

But none of that fazed Pistol because, to paraphrase the Hollies' smash hit that peaked at #1 on the South African Springbok Radio charts in mid-1974, "Sometimes all [you] need is the air that [you] breathe."

I met Pistol when he was trying to round up a team at Ivy for the Club Flag Football League. Which would take some skillful horse trading, because Ivy had so few Big Men. Eventually, after agreeing to type two term papers and a senior thesis to round out the squad, he sealed the deal. Which was no great sacrifice for Pistol because he could type 90 words a minute. Of course, he could. Pistol could do anything. And he did everything fast.

It was a motley crew of shapeless bodies that lined up on opening day against Dial Lodge, the most muscled-up of the mesomorph clubs on the street. In a gesture of mercy, Dial's captain suggested we forfeit and mix up our teams for a fun scrimmage. "No, thanks," Pistol said. "We're going to beat you." If the great Spanish writer Cervantes had ever met Pistol, the world would never have heard the name Don Quixote.

The Club League played a novel brand of razzle-dazzle flag football that permitted unlimited forward passes from any point on the field. However, most teams limited their offense to the traditional rules of football. Maybe they just didn't have Pistol's imagination. Like Feynman, he could see the Cornell logo in the middle of the plate spinning at warp speed. He recognized how the razzle-dazzle rules made the game like basketball, his specialty, and played it to his advantage.

"Everybody spread out and go long," he instructed in the huddle. Pistol dropped back in shotgun formation to receive the first snap and waited for the Dial defender to rush him. When he reached for Pistol's flag, he deked him out, blew past him and ran straight downfield.

Now, with the ball in his hand and the rest of the Philosophers spreading out over the field ahead of him, it was like leading a six-on-five fast break in basketball. Except he didn't have to dribble. Sooner or later, some defender would have to leave his man to stop Pistol. And when he did, he would toss the ball over his head to the now-open receiver— the razzle-dazzle flag football equivalent of an easy alley-oop pass on the hard court.

Dial responded by trying to defend him with two players, forcing Pistol to come up with a new play. Which was the same as the old play, except he told me to line up wide and stay in. I did as I was told, and when the two defenders rushed him, he flipped the ball out to me and ran downfield. I caught the ball and passed it back to him ten yards into the secondary where he hauled it in without breaking stride. Now it was a five-on-four fast break.

That was the extent of our playbook for the year, and we rode those two plays into the championship game against Cottage Club where we came away with a one-to-one tie. An unimaginable cosmological event that left the fate of the universe in doubt. At least to the Club Football League players at Princeton.

When basketball season rolled around, Pistol committed to typing a second senior thesis to form a team. When we showed up with five players, the referee asked what we would like to do if somebody got hurt. "We'll play with four," Pistol said. We only needed one.

Pistol dropped three in a row from thirty and then delivered a perfect no-look, cross-court, bounce pass to me from half-court for an easy layup. Just like the real Pistol Pete. He had all of Maravich's moves. The flips. The curls. The underhand slingshot. And the pull-up jumper he could drop silently through the net from the most distant points of all Mercer County's twelve vibrant municipalities.

There was a certain vaudevillian quality to the way the puffed-up chests from Tiger Inn deflated as they realized they were in for a real game. What began as a fist-bumping band of brothers quickly deteriorated into a bickering, finger-pointing dysfunctional family trying to stop Pistol. We won every game and coasted to the championship. Once again, the universe shifted.

After the season, Pistol arranged for us to play the Princeton first-year team. We held it close against a team that featured three future varsity standouts. But lost a close one, 76–70. Pistol scored 53 points. After the game, he chatted it up with the first-years' coach and the respect and affection they had for each other was palpable.

"You're pretty tight with that coach," I said to him at dinner.

"Yeah, we're good friends."

"So, how come you don't play on the varsity?"

"Oh, no," he replied, as if suddenly discovering he was wearing two different socks. "Carril would never let me anywhere near his team. He hates me."

Pete Carril was Princeton's Hall of Fame basketball coach who led the Tigers to thirteen Ivy League Championships, eleven NCAA Tournament berths, and two NIT bids over a thirty-year career. He is the only NCAA basketball coach to win more than 500 games without the benefit of athletic scholarships.

How could a guy as talented as Pistol, a "high character" guy who didn't drink, smoke, swear, judge others, or draw attention to himself get on the wrong side of a basketball legend like Carril? Of course, it was the system that shot the Pistol down. The famed Princeton Offense. Pete Carril's highly disciplined half-court scheme that spreads the floor to create opportunities for lay-ups off backdoor cuts and picks on and off the ball.

The Princeton Offense was memorialized in Pete Carril and Dan White's book *The Smart Take from the Strong: The Basketball Philosophy of Pete Carril.* It was what enabled the Tigers' non-scholarship athletes to compete against stronger, faster, more athletic teams. And it made every game more of a parable than an athletic event: David and Goliath on the hardwood.

From the Triangle Club kick line to the public policy grinds at what was called at the time the Woodrow Wilson School of Public and International Affairs, and even the *Paris Review* wannabes, Tigers of all stripes would pack Jadwin Gymnasium to witness the unfolding biblical significance of the evening. All eyes were on the Princeton Offense—the sling designed to slay the giant.

The Princeton Offense has been described as a "perpetual motion machine," though, to a guy like Pistol, it was more like a perpetual slow-motion machine. Because Pistol did everything fast. He ran fast. He passed fast. (Typed fast.) And scored fast. But there was no room for fast in the deliberate Princeton Offense that was designed to take time off the clock and reduce the other team's number of possessions.

Pistol made the innocent mistake of bringing a gun to a rock fight, but there were no firearms allowed in the Old Testament. And that's how young David became King of Israel instead of the Pistol—the greatest Tiger baller never to stand for the national anthem in Jadwin Gymnasium.

In a much-deserved storybook ending to Carril's great career, just days after announcing his retirement, his 1996 team defeated the defending national champion UCLA

The Pistol: My G.O.A.T. Classmate

Bruins 43–41 in the first round of the NCAA tournament on a backdoor layup. One of the Princeton Offense's signature plays. The game is considered one of the greatest upsets in college basketball history.

Sports Illustrated called Carril the "blue-collar coach in a button-down league." And when Carril wasn't coaching, it was famously rumored, he could be found at Andy's Tavern, a bar near the Princeton campus that was so seedy, few students dared to cross its threshold.

PAW's online historian Gregg Lange confirmed the legend with a story about a basketball recruit who called Carril at the number on his business card only to get an unfamiliar voice on the other end: "Hello, Andy's Tavern." Carril was so rooted at Andy's, as the story goes, that he had business cards printed up with the bar's number.

Carril's legend, for its PR value to the pricey liberal arts college with the elitist image problem that is Princeton, will live on long after his basketball star has faded. But what was he thinking when he recruited Pistol? "Hey, this kid is fast. I wonder how he would play in quicksand?" Or "Wow, if we can just stop him from doing all the things he does, and the way he does them, he could be really good for us."

And what was Pistol thinking? How did either of these guys see themselves as a match? I don't know what the statute of limitations is on this sort of thing, but if Pistol can find his "good fit" recruiting letter from Carril, he may have grounds for a lawsuit.

One night at dinner, I asked Pistol why he didn't transfer to another school to play basketball. "I came here for the education," he said. "To write a senior thesis." Then he told me about his thesis on the Civil War that he wanted to write in a narrative style, like Bruce Catton.

"That sounds like fun. What does your advisor think?"

"He hates it."

The problem was that the History Department expects a thesis to be a critical history—not a narrative one featuring colorful characters and dramatic sketches. And while Catton received twenty-six honorary degrees from colleges and universities, was a Presidential Medal of Freedom winner, a National Book Award winner, and a Pulitzer Prize recipient, he was not an acceptable role model for a Princeton history major.

"Yeah, he really hates it."

What Pistol really wanted, he explained, was to write his thesis like a Mercury Theatre radio drama. And present it as a three-part series on the university radio station WPRB. Without further introduction, Pistol broke into a dramatic rendering, like the young Orson Welles describing Ulysses S. Grant's attack on Fort Henry on the Tennessee River.

Complete with troop levels, body counts, weather conditions, the height of the river, the inventory of ironclads and wooden ships in Admiral Foote's naval flotilla, and the size of their cannons that bombarded the fort as Grant's troops landed. Masterfully he worked in news reports of Grant's progress from the *Daily National Intelligencer*, the *Washington Chronicle*, and even Grant's correspondence with President Abraham Lincoln.

Everybody at the Philosophers' table and even a few Slickers gathered around as he delivered both play-by-play *and* color commentary for the Union army's Western campaign, as it moved on to the Battle of Fort Donelson, Shiloh, Pittsburgh Landing, and finally the siege of Vicksburg. He blew everybody's mind. It was absolute genius. And completely unusable.

The Pistol: My G.O.A.T. Classmate

The next night, still eager to find a way to snag some airtime on WPRB, Pistol challenged me to a debate. The Grateful Dead vs. the Hollies. "I'll mop the floor with him," I thought. Which is not to say I didn't like "Carrie Anne." But the Grateful Dead had a deeper catalog of music, a greater cultural impact on the era, and—most importantly—the good sense *not* to write or record "He Ain't Heavy, He's My Brother."

Then I remembered, this is the Pistol. The Pistol doesn't lose. Sometimes people won't let him into the gym or the Firestone Library stacks where they keep the Bruce Catton books. But when he gets himself into a game, even if he must drag some sad-sack Ivy Club Philosophers with him, he wins. I wasn't going to mop the floor with him. He was going to mop the floor with me.

And I would go down as the guy who couldn't defend the Grateful Dead against the Hollies in a live format broadcast that would be preserved for all posterity. I did not want to be that guy. So, I turned him down.

And with that, the Pistol was out of bullets. Few came to Princeton as loaded as he. Nobody shot more blanks once they got there. But he never let it get him down. He was never bitter. And he never stopped looking for ways to amuse himself.

The Parallel-to-the-
Ground Steering Wheel

From the prestigious Lint on the Pants Award to two
Club championships, my year at Ivy Club was filled with
honors and accolades. But I was full up on Ivy stories. So,
when a friend, who I will call Bialystok for reasons that will
soon be clear, recommended Terrace Club, I joined.

It would make for the perfect twist in the Tiger narrative I was writing in my head, because Terrace and Ivy
were about as opposite as Princeton eating clubs get. Not
to put too fine a point on things, but Ivy was to Terrace as
Wall Street is to Occupy Wall Street; as creamed chipped
beef is to Moroccan chickpea stew; as Cole Porter's "Brush
Up Your Shakespeare" is to Frank Zappa's "Don't Eat the
Yellow Snow."

While the Ivy mansion is considered a masterpiece
of Collegiate Gothic design, Terrace was the dive bar of
Prospect Street. From its dreary Tudor façade to its hip-
pie-ethos membership, the club was bereft of all the signs of
Slicker life that defined Ivy.

The Parallel-to-the-Ground Steering Wheel

In one way, however, they were similar. Despite Terrace's "let's jump on the couch" vibe, it's average household net worth dropped almost as precipitously when I entered it as it did at Ivy. Except Terrace wealth was less railroads and steel and more like the moneyed-class Tom Wolfe described in his 1970 *New Yorker* article "Radical Chic: That Party at Lenny's."

Terrace was the preferred club for trust-fund Marxists, PBS tote baggers, and Patti Smith acolytes from Manhattan's elite girls' schools Brearley, Spence, and Nightingale-Bamford to go slumming. While their identical cousins who preferred the Ballet Russe and crepes suzette enjoyed a more traditional social life at Cap and Gown.

Such was the environment where I would delight in the virtues of Princeton's recent and historic commitment to co-education, providing me a rich vein to mine for this timeless narrative that takes place on House Parties week-end—Prospect Street's spring bacchanals.

With final exams soon to follow, House Parties was the Tiger faithful's last chance for romance. Closure. New beginnings. Whatever your aspirations, the Saturday evening parties were the main event. It was a night where I would find closure (of a kind), not once but three times. A prolific performance that with this telling, promises to rewrite the book of Princeton House Party lore.

To fully appreciate the story, I am about to tell we must go back to the taproot of the evening for me: the parallel-to-the ground steering wheel that came into my employ the day Bialystok asked me to take over his Student Bagel Agency. The Bagel Agency was one of many student-run businesses founded under the auspices of Princeton Student Agencies (PSA) that was billed as a "hands-on educational program" designed to teach "leadership and business skills."

But was largely a front for students padding their resumes for Harvard Business School.

There was one agency, however, that was the real deal: the Student Hot Dog Agency, also known as the Weenie Man. This entrepreneurial and culinary wonder was PSA's big moneymaker. And proud possessor of a stainless-steel hot dog cart financed by the agency's investment fund.

Students in their rooms at night would hear the carnival sounds of the Weenie Man barking his weenie fare from the walkways in their quad. "Weenie Man, here!" Hungry Tigers with the munchies and anyone craving a good old-fashioned ballpark dining experience would don boots and frock and brave the elements for a late-night nosh.

But Bialystok, ever the visionary, insisted the Weenie Man was on a collision course with destiny. "Bagels beat weenies," he told me. "They just do." On a more cautionary note, he confessed that after a semester of humping bagels around campus, he was making little money and having less fun.

The problem? He needed a cart like the Weenie Man's. The department's director, who I will call Buffet, wouldn't invest in Bialystok's Bagel Agency until it demonstrated proof of concept—as it had failed in a previous incarnation. Leaving Bialystok with no choice but to wheel his product around in, I note here painfully, a purloined grocery cart.

Which raised all sorts of alarms with me, as you might imagine. Not the least being that I promised one grocery cart story and two royalty stories, and I like to keep my word. I was ready to adjourn the meeting when Bialystok said, "They *will* let you use their van, though."

Listening to Bialystok's tales of daily trips to the Princeton Shopping Center to pick up the bagels, with occasional stops at Dairy Queen, was like hearing from your parole board.

The Parallel-to-the-Ground Steering Wheel

So smothering was the penitentiary of campus life by senior year, that the prospect of regular excursions to a suburban strip mall sounded like freedom.

So, I went to talk to Buffet.

Who wasn't very encouraging, as now the Bagel Agency had two failures associated with it. But he let me check out the van that, I elatedly discovered, was equipped with an authentic parallel-to-the-ground steering wheel—just like the ones on the Q31 line I would ride with my grandmother from Flushing to Archer Avenue in Jamaica, Queens, to pay her phone bill on the first of the month.

"Done deal," I said, wasting no time to lock in my ownership of the business that would put my hands on that magnificent parallel to the ground steering wheel—and with it the realization of a childhood fantasy I had almost forgotten. Who said the Ivy League was just a dasher of dreams?

Off to Urken Supply Co. on Witherspoon Street I went, in search of a workaround to the grocery cart problem. Inside, I noticed unsold summer inventory in the form of two Coleman beach coolers on a high shelf in the back that would come to be known as "the Disruptors." I asked the man with the True Value logo on his chest to take them down for me.

"What are you planning on doing with them this time of year?" he asked. When I told him I wasn't going to the beach, he upsold me with two top-of-the line Advantus four-barrel coin changers with slots for pennies, nickels, dimes, and quarters. With an easy-on, easy-off clip. Just like the peanut vendors at Yankee Stadium wore on their belts. Yet another childhood ambition fulfilled.

Next, I needed a staff. Leafing through the *Freshman Herald*, I came across a photo of a Baytown alum posing with a lacrosse stick who I will call Sales Force. I got him on the line only to discover he had just accepted a job with the Weenie Man. But I could tell the Sales Force was strong with him, so I offered him double what the Weenie Man was paying. Ten minutes later, he was knocking on my door with five friends, all wielding lacrosse sticks, who had just resigned their Weenie Man positions. And I filled every shift on my work schedule.

By our first night of operation, the Weenie Man's buns were toast. Sales Force used the light footprint of "the Disruptors" to navigate every nook and cranny of Princeton's byzantine dormitory landscape to bark for bagels *inside* every entryway. Where grinds and slackers alike could grab a snack in their slippers and robes. Leaving the Weenie Man and his shiny clunker of a hot dog cart out in the cold.

Before long, we were selling 2,000 bagels a week and the Weenie Man's distant carnival cries fell silent. Another tale (with apologies to Sir Arthur Conan Doyle) of a hot dog vendor who didn't bark in the night. Through the paradigm shifting use of "the Disruptors," Sales Force spread creative destruction worthy of a Harvard Business School case study across the Student Agency landscape. And a Princeton Student Agencies unicorn was born.

Closure #1: Lilly

As a matter of course, I would pick up the bagels and cream cheese at six and go to dinner at Terrace before delivering them to my prep team at a basement kitchen in Little Hall. As word got out that "Al has a sweet ride," people started asking me for a lift back to campus. One of them was a prim transfer student with jet black hair and alabaster skin who I will call Lilly because she had an extensive Lilly Pulitzer wardrobe.

The Parallel-to-the-Ground Steering Wheel

I have always found the Lilly Pulitzer collection a little intimidating. But there was something different about this Lilly. Whether she was wearing a shift, swing dress, or scalloped skort, it was always wrinkled. Which I liked. She also wore Pulitzer in the winter. I took that as a sign she didn't care what other people thought. As I'm sure you already know, I liked that, too.

That said, it was more than negligent dry-cleaning habits that brought us together. There were many cliques in Terrace. and because Lilly and I were both new to the club, we wound up sitting with other newbies. After a round-robin week of dinners, the newbies started forming their own cliques. By virtue of neither of us finding a home in any of these new social alignments (and because misery loves company), Lilly and I became a society of two.

Thrust together by the whims of the shifting herd, our conversations were little more than a series of digressions held together by nervous chatter about being behind in our studies. But we were always on the same wavelength whenever we lit into other members of the club. More specifically, the other cliques because we didn't know anybody by name.

Everyone was neatly categorized as "Those guys in the corner who, rumor has it, are running a meth lab in the Terrace basement." Or "Those city girls who only eat salad and ice cream and are probably dating professors." And such.

At moments like this, when we were savoring the Moroccan spices and slandering our clubmates, I dared to think ours could be a beautiful friendship. Until one blustery February evening when she asked me for a ride back to campus.

Lilly was wearing a sleeveless Tisbury Shift in Caribbean Green and Wild Strawberry that looked like it had been slept in since June. A season when ladies of her station were

famous for dozing off in Pulitzer. As she climbed into the
seat next to me, I couldn't help but notice she was, as women
often do in summer clothes, showing a lot of leg.

With one eye on the road and the other on the sinewy
left thigh of the pulchritudinous Ms. Pulitzer, I found myself
throwing elbows and shoulders into every up- and downshift
of that van's manual transmission like Gene Kelly on shore
leave in *On the Town*. When I finally gathered the nerve to
glance at her, she was staring at the road ahead, oblivious to
my desperate "dance for the common man." Or so I thought,
because when she finally spoke, she made it clear she hadn't
missed a step.

"You seem to like driving this, I guess you would call
it—a *machine*?"

"Yeah. It's like a city bus."

"Has driving a city bus always been an ambition of yours?"

I mumbled something about municipal transportation,
and she passed sentence on me so prophetic that the sun
hasn't set a day since without it burning a hole in my brain.

"I guess you'll be *moderately* successful."

Lilly may not have been every guy's idea of a nurturing
mate, but there must have been something about pretty girls
in blunt cuts and puckered Pulitzer who can dish a good line
that appealed to me. Because she did. Nevertheless, I figured
I shouldn't fantasize about our friendship going any further.

But the next night, with nary an inviting seat to be found
in the Terrace dining room we wound up together again. In the
weeks ahead, our van rides became more frequent. One Friday
night in spring, I offered to escort her to the top of Little Tower
for a bottle of wine. She said she never knew Little had a tower.
Or that you could go to the top of any Princeton towers.

"How do you get there?"

The Parallel-to-the-Ground Steering Wheel

"The stairs."

After the wine, we went back to my room and our relationship evolved—a couple bases. Which didn't help. We remained an awkward pair. Similar engagements in the weeks leading up to House Parties remained equally unaccomplished. Until one night on the top of Little Tower, she said, "We're very different you know?"

"I do know."

"How so?"

"Well, you're very direct. And at times impatient with nuance."

"And you?"

"Me? I'm all nuance."

"Is that what you think?"

Later that night, my roommate, who I always called Cecil (because he was keen on winning a Rhodes Scholarship), asked me if I was taking Lilly to House Parties.

"I don't see that happening, Cecil."

"Why not?"

"Because Lilly hates me."

"She doesn't *hate* you!"

"Oh, she doesn't know it yet. But she's working on it."

Cecil insisted I ask her. And the next day I did.

"No, thank you," she said.

"She said no?" Cecil gave me that hair-on-fire gesture he used when, as he liked to say, "logic has been ripped from its mother's breast."

"But she's here all the time?"

One would have thought it was Cecil who had been jilted and not me, because he just couldn't let it go. "You can't let this happen," he implored. "You have no idea how much I've been living vicariously through you two."

"Cecil," I said, my hand on his shoulder in a gesture of fraternal love, "It's just one of those things."

A big mistake. Because Cecil, as people so often do when they can't get a song out of their head, proceeded to sing Cole Porter's 1935 hit from the musical *Jubilee* endlessly for days.

And didn't stop singing it until I began to hate the entire Great American Songbook.

Closure #2: Twyla

On other nights, an anthropology major from Los Angeles who I will call Twyla (because she was a dancer), would hit me up for a ride. Twyla was an inveterate culture-vulture, who never seemed to have any homework to do and was always running late for an event at McCarter Theatre, Theatre Intime, or Alexander Hall.

Sometimes her boyfriend, Bradley, who I knew from Ivy Club, would bow out at the last minute and she would offer me his ticket. While I enjoyed Martha Graham and the William F. Buckley–Gore Vidal debate, I didn't really get their whole relationship. But that was their business.

When Lilly didn't come to dinner on House Parties eve, Twyla called dibs on a ride back to campus. At the light on Washington Road and Nassau Street, she asked if I had a date to House Parties. I told her I didn't, and she invited me to go with her. "I can't go to House Parties with you," I said. "What's with you and Bradley anyway?"

She explained how they weren't dating anymore.

Considering this new information, and because of misery's famous love for company, we went to the Terrace party first. Then made our way up and down Prospect Street, stopping in

The Parallel-to-the-Ground Steering Wheel

at Tower, Ivy, Cottage, Cap and Gown, and Colonial. But she didn't drink, and I didn't dance so it was kind of a bust.

After holding up the walls at every club on Prospect Street for far too long, Twyla said she would love to listen to the new Tom Waits album I had mentioned to her. Back in my room, I thumbed my record collection until I found *Nighthawks at the Diner*, removed the record from its sleeve, and lowered the needle on the turntable.

When I turned around, Twyla was on my bed eyes closed in the full lotus position. Jacket off, big clunky hard-to-take-off boots off, slowly rocking her head from side to side. She was, as far as I could tell, in some ethereal place where the eternal goddess energy is said to reside and very close to full lateral flexion. Which weirded me out a little.

But she seemed so happy in my crib that I shrugged it off. Because *mi casa es su casa*, right? When Tom Waits got to the end of "Emotional Weather Report," she opened her eyes and purred, "So-o-o-o good."

"Tom Waits or those neck things?"

"Both." She patted the bed and motioned me to join her. "You look like you could use a neck massage.

What does it say about me that when Twyla said, "neck massage" I heard "sex." Being a dancer and all, it was entirely possible her offer was merely a professional courtesy. They do all sorts of purely therapeutic stretchy things in warm-ups, right? On the other hand, as it *was* House Parties, I couldn't help but think she might be making something of a bawdy overture.

I had never known Twyla to speak in code before, but I found myself running through a checklist of moral questions I might have to answer for on the odd chance that was her intention.

The B-Side of Paradise

The Moroccan chickpea stew from my last meal with Lilly, after all, had barely grown cold. Despite the recency of our affair's demise, however, I quickly dispensed with this concern as I had seen her change of heart coming long before she did. And it wasn't my fault she wasted so much time struggling with the obvious, that she despised me.

Besides, in the unlikely event that Lilly's feelings toward me might change again, I would only be doing her a favor. As for the Bradley and Twyla matter, I still found it a little prickly. But morally, that was Twyla's problem.

So, I was all in on the neck massage.

Then the phone rang. And, of course, I had to answer it. Because in those days before voicemail and text messages, when anyone called you on the phone, you answered. There was no other option. Somebody on the other end might be dying or need directions from the Long Island Expressway to your house.

"Hello Mrs. Pulitzer." I said summoning all the poise I could muster. "No, I did *not* know that Lilly was home with you for the weekend. Is everything all right? Yes, it's always good to catch up on some mother-daughter time.... And please convey my regrets to Lilly that I was unable to attend House Parties with her, as well.... I look forward to seeing her at the club on Monday night, too.... Thank you for your concern.... A pleasant evening to you, too."

Whoa...

It was like *This Side of Paradise* was calling *The B-Side* from beyond the grave.

"I think I should go," Twyla said when I hung up. Seeing that she already had her big clunky hard-to-take-off boots back on, I figured I shouldn't stand in her way. Yet, I felt like we almost had a moment, and I couldn't let it pass without asking.

"Twyla, have you ever noticed the steering wheel in the van?"

"You mean because it's flat?"

"Yeah. Like a city bus. What do you think of it?"

"I don't know. Nobody takes the bus in L.A."

Closure #3: Sophia

I had always imagined House Parties would include a trip up to Little Tower. I just didn't expect to be alone when it did. Even with Lilly and now Twyla out of the picture, the compulsion was strong, and I started my ascent like I was keeping an assignation with myself. At the top, I opened the door to reveal I wouldn't be alone, after all.

There, leaning over the embattled parapet tilting to the full-flower moon of spring was a vision of loveliness. Had she been a figment of my imagination, she would have betrayed my conventional sense of beauty. All the same, standing there barefoot in her yellow cocktail dress, wrinkled in all the right places, she could have been my mind's own creation.

"Do you think it's a sign of our oppressive patriarchy that we see a man in the moon instead of a woman?" she asked, without turning her gaze from earth's only natural satellite.

"Ah, but we only see one side of the moon. There might be a woman on the other…"

"She's still invisible."

"Yet, there are over two hundred moons in our solar system alone. Many, perhaps all…."

"Same problem."

"Well, maybe someday we will have an oppressive matriarchy, and we will all agree there's a woman in our moon."

"Are you patronizing me?"

"I'm trying."

Only then did she turn to face me, and she was Disney Princess–beautiful. Not Snow White or Aurora beautiful, more like Jasmine. Still, it was the kind of beauty one could only expect to find at the top of a medieval tower. Which basically was where we were.

"I see you went to House Parties. Did you have fun? Did you see the guys? Did you have a date?"

"You know, one would think that setting aside a weekend each year where everybody has to have a party would be a good idea."

"I like that. Do you dance?"

"Miserably."

She put one hand on my shoulder and held the other out for me. "Let me show you a basic quickstep." After we nailed a few "slow, slow; quick, quick, slows," she said, "Okay. For real this time." Then, in a manner of accompaniment, she began to sing "Just One of Those Things." That insouciant ode to one-night stands from Cole Porter's 1935 musical *Jubilee* that Cecil had been driving me mad with for the past week.

"Why did you pick that song?" I heard myself say.

"Don't you like Cole Porter?"

"I used to."

"Oh."

There we were, still in our dance embrace but not dancing. Gazing into one another's eyes. In the moonlight. Barefoot. Yellow party dress. Wrinkles.

"It's okay," she said raising her lips to mine as I hesitantly lowered my face to hers.

Many years later, another powerful and confident woman offered me sage advice that would have served me well that night. "When they say, 'yes,' *stop selling!*" Of course, she was talking about advertising, but I suspect it's the same, even with Disney Princesses on medieval towers. Anyway, I wish I knew then what I know now. Because if I did, I would never have asked my next question.

"Do you have a name?"

"Sophia."

"Do you have a last name, Sophia?"

"Safavieh."

"*Safavieh?*" (a beat) "Do you have a brother here?"

"Tony is my cousin. Do you know him?"

"No! Don't know him. Know *of* him. But he doesn't know me."

"How do you know that, if you don't know him?"

Reflecting on that night with the distance of time, when I had the chance to kiss the princess—I should have just KISSED THE PRINCESS—and dealt with the whole kidnapping issue later. Or, I could have confessed to the Purloined Grocery Cart incident up front. She might have thought I was gallant for doing so and might have wanted to kiss me even more.

But there was no getting around the fact the evening just kept getting more complicated. Besides, if I could trust Mrs. Pulitzer, Lilly was expecting to see me on Monday. So, I mumbled my apologies and requested yet another rain check that would never be cashed.

I counted every step of the four flights of stairs from the top of Little Tower to the bottom. Of course, I lost count halfway down. But that's not why I retraced my steps back to the top. Princess Sophia was barefoot in yellow, searching for the woman in the moon, just as I had first seen her—when I popped the question.

"Sophia, do you know those steering wheels they have in buses that are perpendicular to the ground?"

Then she turned to me for what would be the last time.

"I *love* those things," she said. "I *always* wanted to try one."

"I thought you might say that."

And that was closure number three on my epic House Parties weekend on *The B-Side of Paradise*.

Ode to a Tiffany Bagel

Sunday night was the Student Agency Annual Dinner at Prospect House. Somewhere between the rubber chicken and the Baked Alaska, Buffet rose to the podium and talked about the educational benefits the program offered campus entrepreneurs. "Nobody," I recall him saying, was "prouder of the program than President Bill Bowen himself." Who, of course, was not there.

The final business of the evening was announcing the Student Agency of the Year Award. And for the first time in its history, it went to a provisional agency. Mine. Up at the podium, Buffet handed me a glass Tiffany paperweight in the shape of a bagel. My second "Major University Award" in the space of twelve months. Then he shook my hand.

Some might consider that crystal beauty that still sits atop the lab results and 1099s in my inbox as a symbol of achievement and a source of pride. Others might see it as small compensation for, or even a painful reminder of, the three daggers to my heart I endured on House Parties weekend.

But I had begun to see my life as an unfolding narrative, measured in plot points and metaphors. And from a literary

The Parallel-to-the-Ground Steering Wheel

perspective, House Parties couldn't have been more perfect. Such was the way I measured the pros and cons of my life by the senior year of my most spectacular Ivy League career.

All-White Funk Team

Ninety-five percent of Ivy League students graduated in the top 10 percent of their high school classes. Yet, it's a statistical certainty that fifty percent of them will wind up graduating in the bottom half of their college class. You can trust me on this. I've done the math. My point, if you haven't already guessed, is that no one turns winners into losers quite like the Ivy League.

Of course, not *all* Ivy League losers are *total* losers. Witness the three "Major University Awards" I won despite flirting with the academic median myself. Even Type A personalities at the top of the class learn about failure. Although they experience a special kind of defeat from their reach exceeding their grasp. A noble failure optimists call a necessary step toward success. Cecil, my junior year roommate, was a case in point.

What makes his story so painful to tell was that he whiffed on the brass ring (his quest for a Rhodes Scholarship) the same day I collected my third "major" and most cherished university sanctioned award. My unanimous selection to the

All-White Funk Team

All-White Funk Team at Dillon Gym. As if that wasn't bad enough, Cecil was there to witness the award ceremony.

The "Rhodes" is the University of Oxford's most celebrated international fellowship granted to students who have demonstrated academic achievement and moral leadership. Leaders who have what it takes to forge bonds of mutual understanding between peoples and nations.

Cecil was a legit candidate, and he was in the right place to snag one. Princeton has produced more Rhodes Scholars than any other college, except Yale and Harvard. And the numbers faceplant after that. Fourth-ranked Stanford has produced less than half, and sixth-ranked Dartmouth barely a third as many Rhodes Scholarship winners.

Cecil was one of those summa cum laude types who was plugged in to current events; foreign affairs; what they call "public policy" in Washington, D.C.; sports; and popular culture. The type who could bury his nose in books all day and still catch the historic debut of *Saturday Night Live*. Which I caught up with on week three, thanks to him.

Still, it was hard to get my head around the idea that someone my age whose rational brain—the part we use to set goals, plan, and problem solve—was still five years away from full maturity, could ask themselves if they have the moral character to lead humanity to a better future, and answer "yes." Stranger still was that someone who could, would be my roommate.

In any event, no one just wakes up one day and decides their destiny has historic value. One must be born into that line of work. Enter Cecil's father, an Ivy leaguer in his own right, and a true slice of Americana.

Cecil Sr. served at one time or another as president, chairman, or trustee of a dizzying number of local, county, state, and regional civic organizations: his church, the chamber of commerce, bar association, board of education, veteran's council, a museum, and his Cornell alumni club. He reached the height of his career when he became president of the National Association of State Boards of Education and was appointed by President Ronald Reagan to the Intergovernmental Advisory Council on Education. Just the kind of guy who might have a son prepared to forge bonds of mutual understanding around the world.

What makes Cecil more sympathetic than the average story of influence and privilege was that within Ivy Club, where the cream that is said to always rise to the top is stored, he was just some hayseed from a bygone era. A long time ago, his hometown was an important agricultural and industrial center. But that was in the days when copper was king and pack animals had only recently given way to inland water transportation.

By the 1970s, his proud city, located between two rivers that connected the Great Lakes to New York City, was a place that baby boomers who were motivated enough to take the SATs left and didn't look back.

But the politically savvy understand that one Cecil's wasteland is another Cecil's ticket to the United States House of Representatives. So long as there was still a lower house of Congress, brains continued to drain out of the region of his birth, and his family held local sway, Cecil would be uniquely qualified to fill any power vacuum that came his congressional district's way.

As he once explained, he had two paths he could forge in life—after presumably gaining admission to one of the top five law schools. One was to work at a white-shoe corporate law firm in New York City and have a nice life. A prospect he viewed with some ambivalence but didn't rule out. "Because, you know, the money."

The other was to return to his hometown and run for Congress. Then he twisted up his face, tilted his head, and sucked in air through the corner of his mouth. This was his way of conveying the tortured calculus of his life. But that day, I flipped the script and gave him a lesson on how the mathematics of movement worked in my family.

Starting with what I learned at the knee of my Uncle Dominick, who used to grab me by my cheek when I was a little boy and advise me, at all costs, to avoid road work. With all the wisdom of a man who has known the world of construction from inside the sheltering walls of a building, he would say, "Whatever you do, stay away from highway construction. Those poor bastards freeze in the winter."

The summer before my first year at Princeton, Uncle Dom got me a job working with his construction crew. Every morning on our ride into Long Island City, I would get the "poor bastards" talk in case I forgot it from the day before. I'm not sure what the rest of the cement masons did all day but when we arrived, my uncle would secret me away to some distant floor far from where any real construction was going on. He'd hand me a long-handled cement scraper and tell me to have my way with the blisters and popouts on the concrete floors.

Then I wouldn't see anybody until lunchtime when I would join the crew in the mason's "lunchroom." There we would sit on chairs made from stacks of 80-pound bags of mortar mix, eat sandwiches off the 50-pound pails of concrete patch we used for tables, and thank the lord for inside construction.

Every now and then, my uncle would come around and tell me to hole up in the bathroom because his union supervisor was on-site and heading our way. Another virtue of building construction, because on the highway there's no place for nepotism to hide.

If Cecil grew up with the seal of the United States Congress in his head, I grew up with a No Roadwork sign in mine. Like one of those No Parking signs with the red circle around the letter P and a diagonal line running through it. Except mine had a yellow Caterpillar Road Grader on it. Uncle Dom wasn't the only one sounding the alarm on outdoor labor. The No Roadwork sign was virtually our family coat of arms.

One Sunday after church, I received my first economics lecture, sitting around a table of cold cuts. It was a rare occasion when the Italian and Norwegian sides of the family broke bread, salami, and pickled herring together. But that day, I was double-teamed by Uncle Dom and Uncle Olaf. Olaf had his own cushy sinecure as a Group E Structure Maintainer in the New York City subway. That's the way he viewed it anyway since it was mostly warm and dry down there. And by his account, it beat the work conditions aboveground hands down.

Dom and Olaf detailed the hazards of road work for me, each explaining how they applied equally to other outdoor occupations where one is exposed to the elements, like line work, mining, quarrying, and oil and gas exploration. These career paths put a tremendous toll on the body leading to higher health care costs, increased sick days, and a shortened career. Dramatically decreasing your Social Security payments for the rest of your life. Making indoor construction or subway plumbing for that matter the gift that keeps on giving.

"Doozsh," Cecil said as he grazed the side of his head with the palm of his hand. Sharing family stories with Cecil was one of my fondest Princeton memories. But it was not the Cecil who was groomed for world leadership that I thought was so great; it was the Cecil who could cut through my elaborately embroidered ironies and say, "Doozsh."

"Doozsh," he once explained, "is the sound of the incomprehensible meeting the unimaginable." It was also the passage to Cecil's soul. A Chaucer scholar, his greatest gift was his empathy for the human condition. Something he could apply to popular music as well as Middle English literature.

And I am grateful to him for introducing me to Tom Waits' "(Looking for) The Heart of Saturday Night," Leo Kottke's "Pamela Brown," and John Prine's "Sam Stone"—three songs about pathos, disillusionment and unbridled desire that Cecil had a line on like no one I knew had a line on anything.

Cecil's superpower was his ability to spot human despair in life's smallest details. You name the misery and Cecil would find it if it was hidden under a rock. Yes, he had his life mapped out for him. Two lives, in fact. Neither, however, could feed his soul like literature.

"You know, Cecil," I said to him, as we gazed into the dark abyss of our future, "you may have two paths mapped out for you and I have none, but I'm the lucky one. Because I get to make my life up from my own imagination."

"Doozsh."

The Jack of Hearts Bong Toss

Cecil tried to be a good influence on me. One day, maybe because I wanted his approval, I decided to dedicate myself to getting straight-A grades. One semester of excellence would make him proud and satisfy my quest, if only symbolically, for my third "major" award. Cecil was thrilled with my plan and even offered some sound advice.

"Well, if you want to pick up your grades, you could start by, you know, studying sometime." That was Cecil in a nutshell, caring, yet practical.

The first step in my academic recovery was to face the fact that I was a terrible procrastinator, too easily distracted by campus diversions. Be it a movie, a concert, or a basketball game, it didn't take much to get me to drop what I was doing and tag along. Even when there was nothing happening on campus, I could always find novel ways to avoid hitting the books.

Such as trying to follow the plot lines in Bob Dylan's "Lily, Rosemary and the Jack of Hearts" while tossing a football between two bongs without spilling the bongwater on the rug. The Jack of Hearts Bong Toss was a procrastinator's dream—a game of skill requiring mental and physical dexterity, played in a state of constant alarm. That mung-y bong water was always just one bad toss away from funking up the entire room, if not every entryway of the sprawling Little Hall.

It spawned a round-robin tournament that lasted for two days. Ending in a draw, when nobody could answer the tie-breaking question: "Who was with Big Jim but was leanin' to the Jack of Hearts?" Since there was no winner, we all pitched in to replace the rug at the end of the competition.

Sometimes Vonn and I would go to Firestone Library to watch Professor John Nash—the Nobel laureate in economics and subject of Ron Howard's Academy Award–winning movie *A Beautiful Mind*—pace large looping figure eights on the lobby floor. Something he could do longer than we could pretend to study. His orange high-top Converse sneakers rhythmically squeaking on lift-off and landing like he was auditioning for the nineteenth chair in Steve Reich's "Music for 18 Musicians."

Nash was a cautionary tale for us because we didn't know he suffered from schizophrenia. The word on campus was that he had blown his mind thinking abstract thoughts for the defense department, which sounded plausible to us. We would check him out whenever we needed a reminder about what can happen if you study *too* hard. Or work for the DOD. There was always something worthwhile to do, and someone to do it with, if you really didn't want to study.

So, I developed a time-management system that would embrace my inner procrastinator rather than condemn him. It revolved around what I called my Guilt-Free Social Hours (GFSH): a three-hour window every evening when I had to accept all invitations that came my way.

Around midnight, when the campus lights began to dim and GFSH was over, I would hit the books until six a.m. Crash until noon. Go to Harry's Luncheonette for breakfast. Take in my afternoon classes. Play basketball at Dillon Gym. Pick up the bagels and go to dinner at Terrace. And then it would be time for GFSH again.

Everything was going like clockwork, and I was on top of all my classes until a week before midterms when Joseph Heller's *Something Happened* came out. In his review for the *New York Times*, Kurt Vonnegut called the book "astonishingly pessimistic" and marveled over Heller's "depictions of utter hopelessness" and his ability to "deal with unrelieved misery." Naturally, I couldn't put it down. And because it is a long book, it left me scant time to attend to other matters, such as classes, reading assignments, and at least one midterm exam.

The B-Side of Paradise

"Oof!" Cecil said when he saw my midterm grades. "What happened?" Before I could explain that *Something Happened* happened, he found another part of my life to question. "And by the way, what kind of courses are these? The Sociology of Deviance? Literature of Exile? Comparative Imperialisms? And Buddhism? You're not majoring in American history; you're majoring in yourself?" Technically that was not true.

"What were you thinking when you chose these classes?"

Of course, I wasn't really thinking anything. Not in the conventional sense of how one might shape a curriculum within a chosen major at a leading university. The truth is, I picked courses the way I sifted through the record bins at the once ubiquitous music retailer Sam Goody. A cool album cover, or a quirky band name like Mott the Hoople or the Flying Burrito Brothers was all it took for me to lift an album out of the bin and walk it up to the checkout counter.

Which was exactly what I did when I saw the disturbing illustration of madness personified on King Crimson's *In the Court of the Crimson King*, and the song title "21st Century Schizoid Man" at the top of the track list on the back. An album that just happens to be considered an iconic work of the Progressive Rock genre today. Since I wasn't disappointed then, I figured what worked for rock and roll might work for academics, too.

And nobody ever tried to tell me otherwise...until Cecil—who nearly popped an artery when he discovered my course load required 1,200 pages of reading per week. Cecil showed me these little numbers at the bottom of each class description in the course manual. "Do you know what these numbers mean?"

I didn't even know they were there, but apparently they indicated each course's weekly required reading. I suppose that could have been useful information when I was selecting my classes. At least that's what Cecil was suggesting.

"Nobody can keep up with twelve hundred pages a week. Nobody."

"Well, it's too late now..." We agreed.

He suggested I focus on the supplemental reading—the scholarly articles supporting each week's reading assignment. Those articles often frame the questions on exams, he explained, and I would be well prepared if I just read *them*. But you couldn't take those articles out of Firestone Library and my study hours, in my new time management system, didn't start until it closed. So, Cecil's idea didn't go anywhere. And neither did my grades.

Besides, I liked reading the books. I did my best and I never felt that I missed anything. Like I told Cecil whenever I got an exam back, "I understood everything. I just couldn't prove it."

"Doozsh!"

Cecil Gets Hosed

When Cecil received his rejection from the Rhodes Scholarship committee, I was lacing up my Nikes to head over to Dillon Gym for some pickup basketball. I invited him to tag along, and, on the way, I noticed a bounce to his step I hadn't seen in a long time. Like he was freed from the pressures of trying to run the world.

We had some decent games that afternoon, and between them I explained the anthropology of the Dillon Gymnasium pickup basketball scene to him. It started organically when we were approached by an earnest-looking gym rat who was trying to form a team.

"Wanna run? I need two."

"Sorry, I got next on court three and my team is here."

"What was that all about?" Cecil asked.

I explained how teams were formed at Dillon Gym. The people walking around saying, "Wanna run? I need one." Or two or three… Meaning that they have reserved the next game on one of the four courts and are recruiting a team. People walking around asking "Need one?" are looking to help you fill your roster.

Everybody was always trying to get lined up with the best talent because winners hold court and losers sit. But you couldn't be obvious about it because it was considered unsporting to turn down either a "Wanna run?" solicitation if you were available. Or a "Need one?" if you didn't have a full squad. Sometimes to hold court and get three or four good runs in before dinner, you had to be prepared with some savvy pretexts. Such as…

"Gotta stretch first. I'm coming off a hammy."

"I'm gassed. Gotta sit one out."

"Wait, I thought *I* had next on this court."

That was a neat bit of subterfuge, sort of like a Jedi mind trick, because once you finally gave in and let the guy have his court, he wouldn't bug you to play with him anymore. "But he looked like he could be pretty good," Cecil said.

Cecil wasn't wrong. This guy was pretty good in a pick-up basketball kind of way. But I found his game aesthetically displeasing. Annoyingly so. He looked away on every pass he ever made. As if it makes it a "no-look" pass if you throw your head up with wild-eyed alarm *after* the ball is already out of your hands and on the way to its target. He also had this uncontrollable habit of tilting his head to the side on his jumper. It was a telling intramural tick—a sure sign he never made it past J.V. in high school.

"I would rather lose than win that way," I told Cecil.

Just then, the gym got quiet and players from the far courts drifted away from their games and moved to center court. "What's going on?" Cecil asked.

The Celtics were playing the Lakers. Or at least that's what I called these two pickup teams who to a varying degree of discipline always tried to play together. The Lakers were a changeable cast of brothers who congregated around Ice Man, a six-eight high school player from Trenton. Ice Man had a sweet finger roll like the original Ice Man, NBA star George Gervin. I often played against them, and we would always lose but it was good ball, so I didn't mind.

The Celtics, on the other hand, I hated. They were five slices of Wonder Bread from wherever they bake Wonder Bread. They never broke ranks. They never let anyone run with them. And they wouldn't run with you, either. No matter how badly you needed a body. But they were the best team in the gym and never lost...except sometimes to the Lakers. Whenever they met head-on, it always drew a crowd, and I would take a seat in the stands to root for the Lakers.

Once, for lack of a better available brother, the Lakers motioned me to play with them against the Celtics. They were a bit aloof toward me at first, but, when they saw that I knew how to maintain court balance, they began to dish me the ball. I hit the game-winner against the Celtics—and boom it was schadenfreude time, the greatest moment of pleasure I have ever derived from another person's misfortune.

Cecil and I watched the Celtics hold court 7–6 that day. When the game was over, we decided to pack it in. On our way out, a brother hopped out of the stands and approached us.

"Excuse me," he said to get my attention. "I would like to inform you that you've been selected to the Dillon Gym All-White Funk Team."

Then he half-turned to his brother-friends in the stands who gave me the thumbs-up, indicating this had been a juried decision and that it was unanimous. "It's been a *long* and *deliberate* process, so…" And then he flashed me his knuckles for a fist bump and said, "Peace out, brother." So, we bumped knuckles and I said, "Peace out."

"That was actually pretty cool," Cecil said. "Do you know those guys?"

"Not really."

"Then that's *very* cool. I mean, those guys have been watching *you* and talking about *you*."

Then I felt bad that maybe I hadn't expressed enough gratitude to the brothers. Frankly, it haunts me to this day that I didn't follow up the fist bump with a dap shake or even a dap hug. But I was gassed. And the award ceremony caught me by surprise. Still, the awards significance, which I regularly work into conversations to this day, just keeps growing with each new telling.

"Maybe you really *are* the lucky one," Cecil said.

Then he got this faraway look in his eyes. The kind that only happens when worlds collide, tectonic plates shift, or A- and B-sides change places. Like when the Beach Boys released "God Only Knows" on the B-side of "Wouldn't It Be Nice." And it wound up being a bigger hit.

Rolling Stone ranked it #11 on their list of the 500 Greatest Songs of All Time—286 spots ahead of "Wouldn't It Be Nice." And Paul McCartney called it the greatest song ever written. THE GREATEST EVER! And it was a B-Side! That's the level of cosmic upheaval I saw in Cecil's eyes that day.

All-White Funk Team

Which is why I always say they should never let a born-and-bred *B-Sider* into a school like Princeton in the first place. People can get ideas from a guy like me. And no Ivy League college needs any ideas from me. I wished he wasn't there to see me receive my third "Major University Award" on the same day he got hosed by Oxford. And I wished I never said I was the lucky one when we were staring into the dark abyss of our futures that day.

Now, to make matters worse, I'm writing his story. Cecil should be writing this book, not me. He's the guy who can find misery under a rock. He knows what it's like to reach for the brass ring. He can tell you about the Ivy League better than me.

Funny thing... I once told this story to some people at the Loews Santa Monica bar on one of my frequent business trips to Los Angeles. They said, "Al, you *do* know the All-White Funk Team is not a real award?"

Can you imagine anybody saying that?

Doozsh!

The
Crash and Burn

Director of Alienation

How is it that *U.S. News & World Report*, no matter what you think of their "Best Colleges" methodology, rated Princeton the top national university in America twenty of the past twenty-two years? When the Harvard brand is as closely associated with the concept of "best college" as Kleenex is with best, well, Kleenex? Or whatever else you call those thin sheets of paper you wipe your nose with during the cold and flu season.

To understand why Princeton dusts Harvard, you must know the Princeton Pitch. Everybody associated with Princeton—from alumni, students, and faculty to the busboys at PJ's Pancake House—knows the pitch.

THE PRINCETON PITCH

Princeton offers the best education because it has small classes, the best professors teach undergraduate courses, and all students are required to complete a senior thesis.

The B-Side of Paradise

Harvard, in contrast, is famous for its celebrity professors who teach graduate courses exclusively. While undergraduates languish in large lecture halls listening to the nasal drone of graduate assistants who hate the students because they know the students hate them.

Ironically, the first time I heard the Princeton Pitch was in Harvard Yard when Haiku George, Doug, and I visited the campus our senior year in high school. There we were—two National Merit semifinalists and me—wandering the Cambridge campus thinking, "Whoa! *Everybody* here is smart." When a tweedy Porcellian descended upon us like Ethan Hawke stepping off the screen of *Dead Poets Society* to give us an impromptu docent tour.

Hawke—we might as well call him Hawke because, for all intents and purposes, he *was* Ethan Hawke—told us he worked for the admissions office. We didn't believe him because of the way he repeatedly trashed Harvard. Which, of course, was part of his calculated charm and we bought his act from curtain to curtain.

Hawke had a way of mixing tour-guide trivia with wry Ivy League–snark that elevated him to godlike status in our eyes. And before the day was out, we came to think of him as the Pagan God of Cambridge Cool, the embodiment of the celestial axis around which all self-aware Ivy Leaguers revolve.

"This is the Harry Elkins Widener Memorial Library. It boasts fifty-seven miles of shelves, and houses over three and a half million books. It was built with a gift from his mother, Eleanor, after Harry's death on the RMS *Titanic*. You might want to consider, before you decide if Harvard is the best place to continue your education, that its academic nerve center is a memorial to a shipwreck. Not just any shipwreck, but history's deadliest civilian maritime disaster."

Director of Alienation

In turn, we were eager to show him that we, too, were godless nihilists, but couldn't muster better than a dumb, "So...how do you like Harvard?" Without further provocation, Hawke delivered a heathen creed that made the entire Ivy League blush that day.

"Harvard is a great place to go to college... But if you want the best education, go to Princeton. The classes are small, the best professors teach undergraduate courses, and all undergrads are required to complete a senior thesis."

There it was. The Princeton Pitch. We travelled five hours from Baytown to Cambridge on a fact-finding mission about Harvard and we got the Princeton Pitch. Of course, that only made us covet Harvard even more than we already did. Princeton-Schminceton, we wanted to be like Hawke: smart, hip, and jaded in Cambridge.

Which brings us to the great climax of every Tiger's undergraduate experience: the senior thesis. For a select few, the thesis is the apotheosis of academic glory. An opportunity to do original research on a topic of one's choosing. A chance to answer the big questions in one's field from a novel perspective. Or maybe even answer questions that have never been asked before.

Top students can burnish their resumes and kickstart their careers with original scholarship worthy of publication. For most Tigers, however, it's just one more joyless slog the dutiful must endure on their way up the ladder of life. But for me, it was the final and longest dark night of the soul in my Tiger career.

There are two major hurdles to clear to satisfy the thesis requirement. The first is picking a topic. During this period, seniors may have trouble tracking their thoughts, and can experience sleep disturbances, depressed mood, and other symptoms associated with early-stage psychosis. The second is writing it, which, symptomatically, is just more of the same, but lasts for eight months.

At first, I didn't lose any sleep over my topic. Because I knew exactly what I wanted to do. Cecil was right when he said I was majoring in myself. The truth is, when I chose courses like the Sociology of Deviance and the Literature of Exile, I was less interested in society's outcasts so much as I saw them as opportunities to psychoanalyze myself for academic credit.

Now, seeing myself as some sort of folk hero, all I wanted to do was write my *B-Side* stories. The way Jack Kerouac wrote about his adventures with Dean Moriarty and Carlo Marx.

With all the conviction of a clear-eyed son of Old Nassau tapped by God, or Old Fitz himself, to define the Tiger narrative, I went to see my advisor. And proposed *The B-Side of Paradise*, the memoirs of a crashed and burned Ivy Leaguer, for my thesis.

But I was a history major. So, that was a hard no.

"The Registrar," I thought. The keeper of academic records, departmental requirements, and Queen Mother of scheduling sleight of hand. She'll know what to do to help me switch my major to Creative Writing three weeks into senior year and still get me out of here on time.

"Funny guy, right?" the Registrar lady said.

"No, I'm serious. I have a plan," I told her.

"I know the routine. You don't like the library. Footnotes are for squares. And you want to write about yourself and your pothead friends." I could see there was no reasoning with her, so I started scrounging around for a new thesis topic.

That night, Twyla invited me to a Lawrence Ferlinghetti poetry reading. I knew about Ferlinghetti. I had even been to his bookstore in San Francisco, so I accepted her invitation. He read from his newest book of poems, *Director of Alienation.*

The title poem follows Ferlinghetti through Macy's department store, where he comes across a mirror, as we all have done, that makes him look fat and frumpy and want to exchange his clothes for some of Macy's clothes. Ferlinghetti describes his shopper's dysphoria as feeling like Charlie Chaplin in clown shoes and a bowler hat with a sign on it reading "Director of Alienation."

He walks us through a succession of paranoid feelings he gets, such as thinking the security guards are watching him, the classic fear someone might discover the hole in their sock, and his powerful compulsion to grope the mannikins. He says he feels like an outsider. And then despairs that being an outsider is "such a cliché."

So, he throws off his clothes, slides down the escalator bare-ass, and climbs between the on-sale sheets on the on-sale beds. Imagining the Keystone Cops running through a Macy's home furnishings department chasing all the alienated people.

From there it's a short leap to the revelation that all Macy's shoppers are alienated "from something or someone, from the whole earth even." The poem ends as the earth reclaims itself from civilization, and returns to wilderness, crickets, and seabirds.

Naturally, I began thinking of myself as the Director of Alienation. And because I was suffering under the delusion that my disaffection might have historical significance, I thought Ferlinghetti's book of poems could help define my thesis topic. Or maybe the poem *was* my thesis topic. I wasn't sure how that would work, but I figured I would let my advisor worry about that. After all, he was getting paid to do this, I wasn't.

The B-Side of Paradise

I brought a copy of *Director of Alienation* to my meeting with my advisor, and plunked it down on his desk as if to say, "See where I'm going with this?"

And he did. A lot better than I did.

"You may have to broaden that out to the whole Beat Generation," he said.

I said, "Oh, yeah. Kerouac. Ginsberg."

"And compare them to the Transcendentalists."

I said, "Hawthorne. Emerson."

"Whitman, too."

"Whitman, too."

"Make sure you spend as much time on the social movements as you do the literary themes." And most importantly, he told me I was to tie it all back to the changing nature of work and the national character as the country moved first from a pre-industrial to an industrial and then a postindustrial society.

"That's what I was thinking," I told him.

"You don't want to short-change the history, or the theory."

"That's what makes it a history thesis."

"American Studies."

"American Studies."

Then he started naming all these books I should read off the top of his head, like he had been working on his own thesis on the same topic. Which, in a way, he was, as later revealed in his 1982 book, *Screening Out the Past: The Birth of Mass Culture and the Motion Picture Industry*, that was informed by many of the same sources he recommended for my thesis. Best of all, I left his office with the following notes, without which all bets would have been off regarding my academic future.

- Henry Nash Smith's *Virgin Land: The American West as Symbol and Myth*, Chapters 1–8 & 12.
- David Potter's *People of Plenty: Economic Abundance and the American Character*, the whole book.
- Herbert Gutman's *Work, Culture, and Society in Industrializing America*, Chapters 5–7, 11, 16.
- David Riesman's *The Lonely Crowd*, the whole book.
- Daniel Bell's *The Cultural Contradictions of Capitalism*, first third.

I wanted to get a fast start and knew if I was going to write an American Studies thesis about the Beat Generation, the first thing I would need was a beret. In short order, I was spinning the parallel-to-the-ground steering wheel in the student agency van heading into Greenwich Village with Lilly.

There I was, jumping the clutch and pushing the throttle like Dean Moriarty leaving Testament, Virginia, in 1948 with Sal in *On the Road*. Heading to New York City to meet up with Carlo Marx. While Lilly was staring out the window wondering if, in retrospect, her mother had really been the best person to go to for guidance about affairs of the heart.

I found the perfect black beret in an army-navy surplus store in the East Village, along with a black turtleneck and peacoat. And I left the store with that incomparable feeling of satisfaction people get after a particularly good day of clothes shopping.

Then it hit me that Lilly needed some beatnik threads, too. She resisted at first but when I explained the look we were going after was Audrey Hepburn in *Funny Face*, she was in. We scored a pair of black capri pants at a vintage shop across the street. And a black-and-white striped Breton top.

The B-Side of Paradise

Finally, we ended our day trip into the great New York City time capsule of the Beat Generation at the West End Bar on Broadway and 114th Street. The famous meeting place of Allen Ginsberg, Jack Kerouac, and Lucien Carr when they were students at Columbia.

We pulled onto campus around dusk and ran into Buffet, the Director of the Student Agency program, and I got busted for stealing the van. Of course, I didn't in so many words *steal* the van any more than I *kidnapped* Prince Tony. But I didn't exactly reserve it, either. Had I checked the sign-out sheet, I would have noticed it was reserved for a Student Agency team-building retreat.

Not only did I miss the retreat, but Buffet and the rest of the Student Agency team had to shuttle three trays of donuts, a two-gallon jug of punch, a two-gallon jug of water, plates, cups, napkins, trash bags, and a folding table down to Poe Field and back—on foot.

It was the dumbest thing I ever did in a career of doing dumb things. I apologized profusely, but it embarrassed Lilly and I could tell that was the last straw. Who could blame her? I was no prize.

I threw myself into reading about Kerouac's dharma bums, Ginsberg's angelheaded hipsters, Whitman's friendly and flowing savage, and Thoreau's men of quiet desperation. Then I began work on my abstract in preparation for my "pitch meeting" with my advisor.

Pitch development season was the most social part of the senior thesis. Everybody at Terrace Club wanted to know one another's topic, hear their pitch, and practice theirs on you. Over the next several weeks, Terrace's rigid social structure collapsed under the weight of its left-bank pretensions—and the basic human compulsion to know everybody's business.

Director of Alienation

I had dinner with Marxists with trust funds, President's Circle patrons of PBS Thirteen, two students who, rumor had it, legally changed their name to Patti Smith, and one of the guys in the corner who, by now I was certain, was running a meth lab in the Terrace basement. All of whom were eager to see if I was half as cool as my thesis topic. Night after night, everybody practiced their pitch on someone new, refining it from the previous night for their next audience.

Soon everybody was a Hemingway, Fitzgerald, or Picasso, and every dinner was Saturday night at Gertrude Stein's. It was a month-long moveable feast, and we were a new Lost Generation trading thesis pitches over Moroccan chickpea stew at the Paris of Princeton eating clubs—the Tudor dive bar, Terrace. All that came to an end like Stein's salon in Vichy France after our advisor meetings.

I went into my advisor's office loaded for bear that day. And I hit him with more jargon in the first two minutes than a White House press briefing. And that's saying something. Legend has it, I used the phrases "polarization of property into the hands of the few," "permanent war economy," "rise of the white-collar salariat," and "subversive tradition of popular culture" all in the same sentence. Without grammatical pause.

By the time I got to the themes of the literary movements, I was exhausted and reduced to one-word sentences. "Individualism." "Spirituality." "Nature." Then I wrapped with my well-practiced and poetical close, "Humanity trying to reclaim the earth like the earth reclaims the land in Ferlinghetti's poem 'Director of Alienation.'"

"You've got it," he said. "Now, go home and write it."

I left his office on a natural high, thinking I may be a real deal historian after all! Until dinner when I compared notes with several other Terrace Clubbers whose advisor pitch meetings ended with the same nine words: "You've got it. Now, go home and write it."

The academic challenge of the senior thesis can be a bear. Yet most students are up for it. And while my, at best, tedious finished product showcased only the occasional grammatically correct sentence and, rarer still, a coherent thought, I was in some ways, too.

But the process of writing a senior thesis is far more demanding than its academics rigors. It requires breaking the assignment down into small pieces—like an engineering project. In those days, the tool of the trade was a stack of common index cards. Assembly instructions called for jotting down ideas relevant to the theme of your thesis as your research reveals them—one per card. Periodically, you sort the cards in a sequence that follows the flow of the argument you want to make. Then start all over again.

While this method was widely accepted at the time, it was too conventional for what I had in mind. In the spirit of honoring Jack Kerouac, who was now the undisputed main character of my thesis, I resolved that I would write it the way he wrote *On the Road*. On a 120-foot-long roll of paper. In one long stream-of-consciousness explosion of spirituality, jazz, and drugs.

Since I didn't know where to get a 120-foot roll of paper, I stapled thirty-five sheets of Eaton Corrasable Bond together in preparation for knocking back the first chapter over Presidents' Day weekend. With ample stock of NoDoz, Entenmann's chocolate donuts, and every Charlie Parker album I could find at the university store, I sat down and waited for my first vision.

When Parker's saxophone kicked in on "A Night in Tunisia," I began writing. Or, as Truman Capote put it, *typing*. In one ecstatic rush of literary criticism and political theory, I filled my first page with powerful insights on the corporate state, Keynesian economics, Ginsberg's *Howl*, and Kerouac's *The Subterraneans*. Then the paper jammed.

I unlocked the carriage, fed the sheet through to clear the jam, and grooved out another page of American Studies to the sounds of Charlie Parker and Dizzy Gillespie on "Salt Peanuts." When the paper jammed again, I tossed my jerry-rigged "roll" aside and started anew on single sheets, determined to recreate Kerouac's method by reloading as fast as I could. That didn't work, either. So, I went to the university store and bought a pack of index cards.

Rather than using them for stringing together ideas, I decided to use them to string together footnotes. I chose footnotes the way I chose classes, which was the way I picked records in a music store. For instance, I saw a line in a poem in Ferlinghetti's *A Coney Island of the Mind* about waiting for the war that will "make the world safe for anarchy."

That was a cool line; it had to be in my thesis. I figured I would find some way to string that between two other cool quotes. And in this way, I would write myself from one footnote to another until the thesis was done. It was also a good way to ensure I was citing enough sources, as I always got docked on papers because they were thin on references. As one professor noted, "I must admit you have some worthy thoughts here, but did you do *any* research?"

Stringing together footnotes without "ideas" attached to them proved to be more difficult than I had imagined. The problem, I decided, was not that they were gathered randomly and couldn't possibly form a coherent argument, but that I didn't have enough visibility into my stack of cards.

I reduced them to thin strips by cutting away the negative

space and was able to lay many more smart scholarly references and hip literary source material on my desk at a time. Which made it easier to rearrange them. And if I had not miscalculated the problem, which of course I had, I should be able to sort them into a coherent sequence. That is, if I could have just found some room on my desk for my typewriter.

I took a trip to Urken Supply Co. on Witherspoon Street where the man with the True Value logo on his chest sent me home with a dispenser of Scotch Magic invisible tape. By taping the strips to the shade on my desk lamp, I was able to clear room for my typewriter. Best of all, I could twirl the shade around in either direction by loosening the wingnut on the lamp harp whenever I needed to shop for my next quotation.

And because it wasn't really a desk lamp, but a statement piece that once sat on my parents' round marble table in the bay window of their house, it was quite large. So, I could get three rows of footnote strips, one for each chapter, more than 100 in all on the shade. With the first row hanging below its lower rim, conveniently at eye level.

My plan was to remove each one after I inserted it into my text, spinning the shade as needed to cue up the next. When the first row was bare, I would be finished with the first chapter. Then I would drop the next row of scholarly oohs and literary aahs down to the bottom rim of the shade. And I would be on to chapter two.

There was one final problem. After ninety minutes, the lamp would melt the magic off the Scotch invisible tape, and the organizational glue to my thesis would drop from the shade. Then I would have to shut down my whole operation. I began working in sixty-minute increments, just to be safe, and would then turn off the lamp and go for a walk.

One night, I was stringing together footnotes in my mind

when I heard someone call out from the street below. I opened my window and saw Lilly in her capri pants and Breton striped top waving me down. Since I still had forty-five minutes of lamp time left, I hastily ran down to see what was up.

Lilly was on her way to the Porn Shop for a Philadelphia cheesesteak hoagie (I assumed, seeing that she subscribed to *Newsweek* and never showed much interest in *Juggs*) and her body language said she wanted company. Since I was always up for some good Porn Shop fare, I joined her. When we got to Nassau Street, we decided to go to the Alchemist & Barrister, instead.

We pounded through a bottle of their cheapest red wine before the waitress returned to take our food order. By the time our Bill Bradley Burgers arrived, we had finished our second bottle and lost our appetite so we just finger fed ourselves the shoestring fries, which were amazing.

That's when I unloaded on her. I said things I never thought of telling anybody. First, I told her I really missed her. She said, "Same."

Then I said, "I don't know why I can't..." And "I really want to try..." And "Wouldn't it be nice if..."

She said, "Same." "Same." "Same." And that was just the beginning. Although everything after that was just variations on those themes.

So much emotional wheel-spinning was happening that neither of us noticed the rain and wind blowing like Charlie Parker and Benny Harris on "Ornithology" outside our window. By the time the thunder and lightning broke, we were the only ones left in the pub and the hostess wanted to go home. She lent us an umbrella and we made our way back to campus with dry heads but wet shoes from a puddle on Nassau Street that was a lot deeper than it looked.

The B-Side of Paradise

As we approached Edwards Hall, I noticed the lamp was missing from my window. Inside, my parents' statement piece and structural core of the engineering project that was my thesis, lay wounded on the ground. Index card strips scattered across the floor. Wet. Curled at the edges. There were 100 2"x 6" monochromatic ink-blue, impressionist watercolors where once proud footnotes stood.

Long story short, all the king's horses and all the king's men couldn't put my thesis back together again. At least not in the same order. Which is why my advisor had to tell me, "Your thesis has more ideas in it than the rest of my advisees combined…. But I couldn't give you a better grade because pages seventeen to twenty should be pages three to six. And three to six should be twenty-eight to thirty-one. While twenty-eight to thirty-one should be in the third chapter, and I can't find anything in your thesis that might replace pages seventeen to twenty." And so on.

My point is, if you have the good fortune to be admitted to both Harvard and Princeton, from my experience, I wouldn't use Princeton's senior thesis requirement as your tiebreaker. No matter how committed you are to getting the best education.

The Night We Outed
Fascists Until Dawn

I may owe the world a big apology. And I want to make it now before someone traces this virtual civil war we are living though back to me. And one final eventful evening in senior year—the night my friends in the Love Suite and I outed more than 500 fascists in the Princeton Class of 1976.

If not for Ersatz Cowboy Joel's relentless networking, this frightful misadventure might have remained graciously hidden in the underappreciated place in our brains where forgotten memories are stored. But when Ersatz called to play the Remember When game, my worst Ivy League nightmare returned like the hooded figures on horseback chasing Peter Fonda in Roger Corman's 1967 cult classic *The Trip*.

The Remember When game is unlike any other in that the longer you play it, the worse you get. (If you live long enough, you'll understand that sentence.) For example, when Ersatz hit me with, "Remember New Orleans?" and then went off about some wild Bourbon Street reunion we supposedly had, I thought he was blowing smoke.

The B-Side of Paradise

And I don't recall *anybody* getting "thrown out" of Madison Square Garden between Dead sets on March 10, 1981. Or *ever* going to see the Dead with Ersatz Cowboy Joel. Though I'll never forget Jerry's blazing runs on that hopped up "Deal" to open the second set.

But he grabbed me in a bad place, like an ill-advised retweet, when he asked, "Do you remember when you said, 'If your head isn't *completely* blown by your *entire* Princeton experience, you're a fascist?'" That's when I knew I had a confession to make and one more story to tell.

It started at dinner on Thesis Deadline Day when Gillis, one of the guys who was rumored to be running a meth lab in the Terrace basement, invited Lilly and me to a party.

"Lilly? What brings you to Terrace Club?"

"I'm here every night, Gillis."

"You're a member here?"

"We've had this conversation before, Gillis."

Lilly and Gillis, as these things seem to go at Ivy League schools, grew up in the same posh, inner ring suburb of a prosperous western Pennsylvania city. They attended the same prestigious private school. Shared classrooms where accelerated courses were taught. And were lab partners in eleventh-grade Chemistry. But now were like ships passing in the night.

"Erp. Erp. My bad. May I join you?"

Dining with Lilly and Gillis introduced me to new levels of social tension I might otherwise never have experienced—even at Princeton. Adding to the raw emotions of this most anticlimactic Tiger deadline day, Lilly clearly did not like Gillis. And his nervous chatter, mood swings, and mental confusion (all classic speed-freak behaviors) put her on edge like I had never seen.

The Night We Outed Fascists Until Dawn

"Are you sure we've met here before? Erp! Erp!"

Then there was the matter of the peculiar word, "Erp!" that he inserted into the conversation to deflect from awkward moments, but more often served to create them. To the best of my understanding, it was inspired by the fictional robot character R2-D2 from the recently released movie *Star Wars,* later known as *Star Wars IV: A New Hope.*

It seemed to mean everything and nothing all at once. It was adapted by his friends who suffered from what psychologists call an external locus of control: the belief that their fate was not theirs to influence, to express the spiritual death they anticipated upon graduation, as they moved into their chosen occupations whether it be chemical engineering, public policy, or Afro-Caribbean music. Erp! Erp!

One might imagine Thesis Deadline Day would end with a big party night. Except most people are too drained to do anything but crash. On this night, Lilly passed (in favor of some early sack time) when Gillis invited us to his My Thesis Is Bullshit But at Least It's Over party at the Love Suite, his four-man apartment-style accommodations in the award-winning Spelman Hall designed by famed architect I. M. Pei. That included four bedrooms, a kitchen for cleaning bongs, a living area, balcony, and bathroom.

"I'm going to catch up on some ironing. And go to bed," Lilly said.

Then she did something she had never done before. She kissed me in public. "Have a good time. I'll meet you at Harry's for breakfast."

For the first time, I found myself looking to a possible future with Lilly. In just a few days I would take her to prom where, because Princeton had this weird tradition of inviting family, she would meet the rest of the Flying Cannoli's.

The B-Side of Paradise

I envisioned, all in the moment her lips pressed against mine, that we could get an apartment in the city where she would work at the Federal Reserve Bank of New York. And I would get a job at an advertising agency. Just like Old Fitz.

I would write *The B-Side of Paradise* and Charles Scribner's Sons would publish it. I even knew young Charley, the old feedbag, from Ivy Club. We never actually spoke, seeing that he was a Slicker. But once he read *The B-Side*, we would click. I knew it. Then I would get story assignments at *Esquire* and the *Saturday Evening Post*—and Lilly and I could marry. Just like Zelda and Old Fitz.

But we wouldn't drink too much and drive each other crazy because after the Case of the Purloined Grocery Cart, I never drank to excess again. Except for that night at Ivy. And the time Trouble was back in town and they had to take me to the infirmary for sixteen stitches. When I almost died because I told them I only had two beers, and they gave me a heavy sedative because I was so squeamish. Why is it always *two beers?*

With my future playing out in my head, I realized Gillis, whose heart was pumping like a drug-sniffing dog, was waiting for an answer from me. But I had mixed feelings. I believed more than ever that Gillis was involved in the manufacture of powerful stimulants that were illicit unless prescribed at the federal level. And subject to first-degree criminal charges in the state of New Jersey.

I was clever enough to wheedle my way out of the Case of the Purloined Grocery Cart, and the Abbreviated Wrestling Match. Still, I didn't want to press my luck with graduation so near, by getting swept up on some "possession with intent to distribute" charge just to go to some meth head's stupid thesis party. But when he told me about his collection of reggae albums from deep-dive Trench Town bands that were "better than Jimmy Cliff," such as Max Romeo and the Upsetters, I had to check it out.

Gillis and I piled into the Student Agencies van, picked up four cases of Rolling Rock pony bottles at Varsity Liquors, and dropped them off at Spelman Hall. Where some Love Suiters hustled the ice-cold ponies up to the party. Then we headed to Edwards Hall to return the van.

On our way, Gillis pulled out what looked like a sheet of stamps commemorating the classic 1950s era DuPont Nylon ad "Your legs are lovelier in nylons." That was part of their *DuPont Better Things for Better Living Through Chemistry* series.

"Cool stamps," I said.

However, when he separated one shapely stem from the sheet, carefully along its perforation, and placed it on the middle of his tongue where it remained for a few minutes, before he swallowed it—I knew he wasn't sending out graduation cards.

"Art? Thesis? Psychedelics?" he said with a grin only a STEM student proud of their corrupt application of a departmental core requirement could occasion. Such was the way I discovered the rumors about Gillis couldn't have been further from the truth. He was never cooking up speed in the Terrace basement. He was synthesizing LSD in the Frick Chemistry Lab.

Through force of habit, I checked my watch when he tore off another glorious gam and offered me a tab of his Frick Lab acid. Noting it was five minutes into my Guilt-Free Social Hours—that critical part of my crazy-quilt Rube Goldberg of a time management system when I had to accept any invitation that came my way.

Duty bound as I was to the practice that saw me through

the completion of my thesis and other academic miracles, I entered the world of psychedelic drugs. As thoughtlessly and recklessly as everything else I had done over the previous four years.

Much as there was a lag before a binge-drinking first-year starts knocking pitchers of beer from the second-floor ring of the Chancellor Green Pub onto the students below, nothing happened from the blotter acid for a while. Until I parked the student agency van, slammed its door behind me, and heard a loud *zap!*

Then in rapid succession, I was blinded by arrows of light shining down on me from the lanterns on Nassau Hall like a Stasi interrogation; deafened by the flat liturgical sounds of the Nassoons flogging "Blue Moon" like a whimpering three-legged dog; and accosted by a pack of Tower Clubbers, fresh off boosting their resumes with strong action words, laughing derisively at the Joker mask that was now gripping my face.

"Uh-Oh. People!" I warned. Like the first day of Orientation Week.

"Not just people," Gillis corrected. "*Fascists!*"

Blinded, deafened, and accosted as we were, we bolted campus, leaving Nassau Hall—the largest stone building in the original American colonies—behind. And regrouped on Nassau Street, where we planned our escape route via University Place, the lonely campus perimeter road that could lead us to a back entrance to the Spelman Hall complex.

Then the cops came. I'm not talking about the proctors, but gun-toting borough police, walking our way and eyeing us like fresh data for whatever quota they were working on.

I was sure the Joker mask gripping my face like a vise now was enough to put me away for life on a Class A felony charge of criminal possession of a controlled substance. Even as Gillis tried to allay my fears with some trumped up theory that "they can't bust you for smiling."

"But I'm *tripping!*" I explained.

"Relax. The drugs are already inside your body…"

I can see how I might have appeared unschooled in the ways of the carceral state to Gillis that night. Who, as an essential condition of his profession, had a greater understanding of the New Jersey Dangerous Controlled Substances laws than I did. But this was my first psychedelic experience. And God doesn't let anyone have this much fun without a little paranoia.

But the cops, apparently having lost interest in the mind-altering experience that was tearing my emotions to shreds, slipped us the old counterintuitive and walked right past us. Reaching into their brown paper bags for glazed donuts, they returned to their squad car.

We hoofed it toward McCarter Theatre, hearts racing like a jail break, pausing only once to hide behind a tree when two students darted out from the Henry Hall arches into a waiting Volkswagen Beetle and disappeared. We didn't stop again until we saw the taillights of the Princeton Dinky clicking down the tracks on its return trip to Princeton Junction, hauling, I imagined, the ghost of Old Fitz inside. Then we doubled back to Spelman from the south side of campus.

"Abandon All Hope, Ye Who Enter"

Further adding to my paranoia was the poster that greeted us on the Love Suite door bearing the inscription over the gates of hell in Dante's *Divine Comedy*. Popular with troubled youth at the time, I should have recognized it for the gallows humor it was for seniors counting down their bitter-sweet final campus days. Wracked as I was by unexplained fears, however, I took it as an ominous warning about the menacing world that Gillis called the Love Suite on the other side of that door.

Paralyzed with every uncomfortable feeling I could think of, I remained rooted to the second-floor landing like Picasso's "Head of a Woman" on the Spelman Hall lawn. I refused to cross the Love Suite's threshold no matter how Gillis tried to coax me inside—where Trench Town was burning bright with the menacing sounds of urban revolution that is *jah jah* music.

Max Romeo's *War Ina Babylon*, the song that transformed his career from hitmaker of puerile songs like "Wet Dream" and "Wine Her Goosie" into the voice of Reggae protest music, was playing at ear-bleed volume. It was a song that described the tribal war brewing on the dangerous streets of the Caribbean island of Jamaica.

And because it had a good beat and was easy to dance to, the floor was filled with various crazies rocking the off-beat rhythm as if dreadlocks were in their DNA. Eventually Gillis returned with a tall lemon-faced blonde who wrapped me in a Steppenwolf love embrace and ushered me inside.

"Everything's cool in the Love Suite," she assured me.

The last thing anyone needs when they're high on Frick Lab acid is a strobe light. With my synapses already firing in strange time signatures, the dizzying strobe effects gave me a case of flicker vertigo that had me groping for structural support.

Finding ballast against a well-placed award-winning I. M. Pei glass curtain wall, I gazed out at the dystopian hellscape of high achievers suffering with locus of control issues. And knew I had fallen through a trap door in *The B-Side of*

The Night We Outed Fascists Until Dawn

Paradise and entered the previously undiscovered tenth circle of Dante's hell.

Word spread that I had been physically assaulted by jack-booted thugs roaming the campus, then narrowly escaped a high-speed car chase with state troopers on the way. One by one, Gillis' friends approached me to offer comfort and support. Which totally freaked me out.

Midway through an LSD experience, the dayglo colors fade, and any hope this will be the night you see the face of God dies. But there are still six hours left to your trip during which you will grind your teeth, massage your ever-tightening temples, and obsess over the gnawing sensation that your stomach is eating itself alive. And, of course, endlessly smoke dope to take the speedy edge off the acid—and drink beer to rehydrate after the pot.

That point came when the proctors made us turn off the music and the strobe light. And the lank, citrusy blonde, who I will call Senora Farquhar kicked off the acoustic entertainment part of the evening. With the sounds of the classic Lord Kitchener song, popularized by the late, great Harry Belafonte "Jump in the Line (Shake, Senora)" filling the air.

The summa cum laude Senora Farquhar had been there and back on the locus of control spectrum. From canvassing for George McGovern in New Jersey's posh Morris County, to singing dreary folk songs like "Where Have All the Flowers Gone" at open mic nights at Café Wha? Before settling in on becoming the world's next Calypso singing sensation and first Celtic superstar Afro-Caribbean singer.

Senora filled space between songs that night with endless guitar tuning and storytelling. During one folksy flaxen-haired Afro-Caribbean interlude, she introduced me to the crowd and related my story like a Joan Baez talk intro.

"We hope you're feeling better now that you're surrounded by friends in the Love Suite," she said in a breathy Greenwich Village folk scene stage whisper.

Then, some Euro History major in a Stetson Drifter who we all suspected was sober, called out, "Was one of those Gestapos that guy who looks like Rolf in *The Sound of Music?*"

Prompting half of the people there to groan, "Oh...*that* guy." While the other half asked, "What guy that looks like Rolf?" That's when Senora pulled out the *Freshman Herald* and passed around Rolf's headshot for all to see. And then that half of the crowd that had previously said, "What guy that looks like Rolf?" said "Oh...*that* guy!"

But he wasn't one of the Tower Club headbangers we saw that night. And with that, the search was on. As Senora feverishly thumbed the pages of the *Freshman Herald,* hunting for the jackbooted thugs who either beat me up or laughed at my Joker mask of a face, depending on who you heard the story from.

Eventually, Senora decided that if we were serious about pinning an aggravated assault charge on the resume-boosting Schutzstaffel slime they had all grown to despise on my behalf, we would have to go through the *Freshman Herald,* one photo at a time. That's how the game Name That Nazi was born.

As one might expect from an Ivy League crowd, there was a strong push to establish some protocols. Half the Love Suiters thought we should use the Potter Stewart pornography standard: "I know it when I see it." But the other half felt if we were all going to be grinding our teeth, doing bong hits, and downing ice-cold ponies for another six hours, we should develop a rubric.

Methodically strumming a progression of chords from the Calypso Rose classic "Fire in Me Wire," Senora led us through a textbook brainstorming session. Everyone called out any idea that came into their heads, until Sober Euro Guy in the Stetson Drifter went off on a tangent about Reichsführer Himmler's interest in occultism and statistics.

After that, we decided we had all the ideas we needed for our Guide to Profiling Nazis. That Gillis then presented to Senora in standard outline format:

I. Telltale Signs You're a Fascist

a. If your pants are pressed or your skirt is pleated, you're a fascist.

b. If your hair saw the bristles of a brush this morning, you're a fascist.

c. If you make it to breakfast before your first class of the day, you're a fascist.

d. If you know what you want to do after graduation and it doesn't horrify you, you're a fascist.

To name a few...

Finally Namedropping Sober Euro Guy in the Stetson Drifter went too far. "Clarification. How many factors makes a Nazi?" Then proceeded to painfully detail a four-tiered ranking system, from Block Leader up to National Inspector to categorize anyone who profiled positive against one, two, three, four or more Nazi behaviors. That's when the Love Suite erupted with a veritable Greek chorus of *erps*.

"ERP. ERP. ERP. ERP. ERP. ERP. ERP. ERP. ERP."

"Too complicated," Gillis shouted.

That's when I said it. The profiling gem that might have been the crowning achievement of my college career, and without which our outing of fascists that night would not have been so thorough but what appears to have been the taproot of this madness that is now tearing the fabric of our society apart.

"If your head isn't *completely* blown by your *entire* Princeton experience—you're a fascist."

Everyone applauded the efficacy of my single factor screening system. Even Obnoxious Namedropping Sober Euro Guy in the Stetson Drifter…who was all over me with "atta boys." And, who I only now recognized, with the fog of DuPont Nylon Frick Lab acid slowly lifting, as none other than Ersatz Cowboy Joel himself. The alumni networking legend who had returned to campus in his BMW to watch his classmate's graduate.

Anyway, we ditched the list and went with my "nowhere for a fascist to hide" algorithm, that with the aid of Gillis' overhead projector (that only a felonious STEM student might just happen to have) enabled us to blow through all 1,100 photos in the *Freshman Herald* in record time. We never found my assailants, but one future Deloitte accounting partner kept a tally. And our class was split right down the middle: 50% fascist/50% non-fascist.

Now the whole world is playing Name that Nazi. Anti-fascists calling grandmothers fascists. Fascists calling anti-fascists, well, fascists. To the point where it has us all reaching for our pitchforks. So, as I promised in my opening, before this whole kerfuffle gets traced back to me, "I'm sorry. I wish I never had that "Uh-Oh, People!" moment. And I wish I could have been more understanding of the Princeton students whose minds were not completely blown.

But even after four long Ivy League years, I was still young…and still kind of stupid. Not to mention that *we were all tripping!* WE WEREN'T SERIOUS!

The Night We Outed Fascists Until Dawn

After that, the party started breaking up. Some people went to the Princeton Golf Course to watch the sunrise. Others took to the kitchen to clean their bongs. Senora asked me if I wanted to go to Harry's Luncheonette and I said, "Sure."

We ordered breakfast sandwiches at the counter and Harry said, "To drink, my friend?" before I could say, "and coffee." Like he did every time I ate there. When our food arrived, Lilly walked through the door looking like a new morning in a crisp freshly pressed Lilly Pulitzer Sophie dress.

Then walked right past us to take a seat six stools down. She stared straight ahead at the hash browns on the flattop like she focused on the road the first time I gave her a ride in the student agency van; she ordered breakfast and coffee to go. When her food arrived, she got up and walked out, stopping only briefly to say, "*Well, I never...*"

Then I remembered our date. And Harry said, "Something else, my friend?"

So, this is how the Ivy League ends. Teeth grinding, strung out on acid, beer, and pot. Blown off by Lilly because she thinks I blew her off for some willowy bleach job of a Calypso singer. And gap-toothed Harry, sweat dripping off his brow from working the hash browns on the flattop smiling down on me. "Something else, my friend?"

I knew I had to explain everything to Lilly. But a line formed in my head that would be the perfect way to end this story if this is where it ended. "The Ivy League always gets the last laugh." And I began to wonder if I was merely recognizing in real time how closely my life conformed to literary conventions or actively fashioning events to fit the narrative, I had been developing for the past four years.

"Wait! Must I *always* sabotage my life for my art?" I

thought.

I ran after Lilly as fast as I could. Dodging traffic on Nassau Street, horns honking, voices braying, "Are you crazy?" as I made my way from Witherspoon Street to Edwards Hall. Where, heart pounding like a John Bonham drum solo, I had to crash. Dragging myself up to my room on the third floor, I threw myself into bed like the Ivy League trash that, let's face it, I had become.

Just then, there was the final consequential knock on the door of my Princeton career. It was the Strong Confident Woman who I hadn't seen since we had exchanged rain checks a year before.

"I love you," she said.

"Really?"

"I had to tell you before we left."

"Really?"

"You didn't know?"

"Yeah, I might have missed that."

She got a job working with some hotshot literary agent and said I could make some money being a second reader— and still have plenty of time to write. Live with her at her parents' pied-à-terre on Central Park West. And something about courtside seats at Madison Square Garden.

Anyway, *that's* how you pick the wrong girlfriend on *The B-Side of Paradise.*

"Al? Are you in there?"

"Lilly?"

"Should I leave?"

"Are you *kidding* me?"

"Um."

Then, to Lilly's credit, she picked the perfect moment to drop the first f-bomb of her life.

The Night We Outed Fascists Until Dawn

"What the fuck?"

"I'll leave."

"No, *you* stay. *I'll* leave.

Alas, there is no Ersatz Cowboy Joel prompt to help me reconstruct what happened next. When I try, there is only Harry's sudsy voice echoing over the clinks and clanks of his stainless-steel turner scraping the hash browns on the flattop.

"Something else, my friend? *Friend? Friend?*"

Something else, Harry? Yes. I want something else. I want to start all over again. Now that I know who I am. Which I thought would be a great way to end a coming-of-age romp through the Ivy League. Until I found this line from Old Fitz at a similar point in *This Side of Paradise:*

"I don't want to repeat my innocence. I want the pleasure of losing it again."

Old Fitz really crushed it with that one.

I have one more confession to make about those Tower Clubbers. I'm not sure if they were laughing at me. Or just laughing.

The Elusive
Math 447 Syllabus

Near the end of finals in my senior year, I got a call from a man who said he was my math professor. "What math class might that be?" I asked playing along with what I assumed was either a prank or a dumb mistake. "Math 447," he replied. "Commutative Algebra."

He told me the final exam was in three days and his records indicated I hadn't attended any classes, including the midterm. Under those circumstances, he took great pains to explain, 100% of my grade would depend on my performance on the upcoming test. And he wanted to make sure I would be there.

So, I explained to *him* that I hadn't attended any of his "Community Algebra" classes because I didn't sign up for them. Whereupon he told me I would have to take that up with the registrar and hung up.

I phoned the registrar's office to address the matter. The lady I spoke with confirmed that I was signed up for Math 447, something both she *and* the math professor insisted on calling "Commutative Algebra." I told her that was impossible, as I would never sign up for any math class. Certainly not a 400-level class like "Communal Algebra" that must have many prerequisites that, if she checked my transcripts, she would find I never signed up for, either.

"Well," she said, "I have your course sheet in front of me. Math 447 is on it. And you signed it."

This I had to see. I walked over to the registrar's office in West College and was greeted by the same lady who daggered my hopes and dreams when I was trying to bail out of writing a history thesis earlier in the year. And she wasn't any happier to see me than she was the last time.

"You, again…"

She showed me the relevant paperwork and sure enough Math 447 was on it along with my signature on the little line at the bottom of the page. "How is it possible I could be admitted to the class when I haven't taken any of the prerequisites?" I asked. She said there was a note in my file that the professor approved my registration, "So, you must have spoken to him about it."

That was also impossible, as I had never spoken to a math professor at Princeton and even if I did, I wouldn't know what to say. "Well," she said, "you must have charmed him because he approved it."

Losing patience with her patronizing tone, and because I had otherwise satisfied all the requirements for graduation, I announced, much to the amusement of the other students in the registrar's office that day, "Okay, he can just flunk me, then. I'm *fine* with that."

She said, "Not so fast," and pulled out my transcripts revealing I would be three credits shy of graduation without the class.

"What happened to The Sociology of Deviance?" I asked. "I signed up for that, too. And I put a lot of time into that class."

"Well," she replied with one of those insincere smiles, "you should have put less time into that and more into the math because you're registered for that and not the sociology."

"Are you telling me the only way I can graduate is to pass this gonzo-level math exam that I never signed up for on just three days' notice and when I haven't taken a math class in four years?" Then she gave me the "I don't make the rules" lecture. That she had to know I was in no mood to hear.

She let me use her office phone to call my Sociology professor who I was sure would straighten everything out. I couldn't wait for the look on her face when my professor submitted my grade. Especially seeing that my numerical average in the class was an 86. That, if I'm not mistaken, would be rounded up to 90, to give me a big fat "how do you like me now" A– for the class.

Much to my dismay, my Sociology professor had already left for the summer. And she was somewhere in the jungles of Papua, Indonesia, accompanying a team of anthropologists and missionaries in what would be the first-ever academic study of the Korowai people who were still using stone tools and living in wooden treehouses. And therefore, unreachable.

I began to see my long and difficult tenure at Princeton rapidly transforming into an endless one, right before my eyes. So, I figured I would just have to take the exam. "How hard could it be?" After all, I was pretty good at math in high school.

At the university bookstore I found the textbook for the "Communist Algebra" class and began to scan its table of contents, which looked a lot more like some unknown sequel to Tolkien's Ring Trilogy than it did a mathematics text. There were chapters on "Ideals in and Modules over Commutative Rings," "Noetherian Rings and Chain Conditions," and "Discrete Valuation Rings and Dedekind Domains." That frankly sounded a little Middle-earth to me.

But there were other chapters on Localization, Completion, and Dimension Theory that, if they meant what I thought they meant, I might be able to handle. I did some quick back-of-the- PJ's-Pancake-House–napkin calculations and figured out by dividing the number of pages in the book (360) by the number of days remaining until the exam (3), I would have to read *about* 100 pages a day.

Which I thought would be pushing things for a dense mathematics text. Of course, some classes don't cover the whole book, so I decided to have a look at the course syllabus before jumping in. I was hopeful that when I did, I might be able to put a dent in that 360 number.

More importantly, there was an outside chance that all those mythopoetic rings topics might not even be required reading, and all I would have to master was "Localization" and "Completion" and such. Which even if I couldn't do the calculations, I could always write an essay on Completion "theory." (That I happened to have a few of my own thoughts about.) And probably rack up enough partial credits to pass the class and graduate.

But all the copies of the syllabus that typically accompanied the books on the shelves, were gone. I returned to the registrar to see if I could get one there. I got my usual lady, and she directed me to the Course Archives room on the third floor with the same dismissive attitude she gave me every other time I had to deal with her.

"I *trust* you'll be able to find it. Ask for Miss Brooks and *have a nice day.*"

I climbed three flights of stairs and navigated a long, seemingly never-ending hallway. Out past where the early nineteenth-century stone floors of West College turned to linoleum and its dull white plaster walls first troweled during the Jefferson administration yielded to that pale-yellow cinderblock common in post-war institutional construction.

A lot like E-wing at Baytown High.

There I came to a room with one of those Dutch doors with the little shelf in the middle. The kind where they can open the top and do business with you without letting you in. Just like the Guidance Department at Baytown High. Inside, the room was nothing more than one long, narrow corridor lined with tan metal file cabinets on either side. I called out to the woman filing papers at the far end and waited for the echo to reach her.

"Miss Brooks…? *Brooks…? Brooks…?*"

"She's out to lunch. Can I help you…? *Help you…? Help you…?*"

"Yes, but first, she wouldn't be the same Miss Brooks who was my Guidance Counselor at Baytown High? *High…? High…?*"

"I don't know about your Miss Brooks," she said, "She's, *our* Miss Brooks… *Brooks… Brooks.*"

What started out as a journey of great expectations took a turn for the worse when I asked about the Elusive Math 447 syllabus. And she informed me, in a matter-of-fact fashion she must have learned from the Registrar herself, that Miss Brooks was *the only person* who can dispense course paperwork to students. Unless I had written permission from my professor. Which I did not.

I asked how long Miss Brooks usually takes for lunch. She said she didn't know, there was a big faculty luncheon at

The Elusive Math 447 Syllabus

Prospect House, and she might be a while. *"If she even comes back at all."*

I was beginning to wonder if *anything* was real anymore. And why I ever came to this stupid school in the first place. But I pushed all that aside because I had already lost valuable time and any further delays, like waiting for Miss Brooks—*if she returned at all*—would make the mountain I felt like I was climbing insurmountable.

What started out as a fifteen-page-per-hour reading assignment was now pushing a rate of eighteen pages. And that didn't allow for the problem sets that I hoped I could avoid altogether if the exam had a heavy emphasis on Localization and Completion. I knew I had to make up for lost time. So, I went to the Wawa Market for a box of chocolate Entenmann's donuts and a quart of milk.

On the way back, I remembered that I would need one of those yellow highlight markers. Once again, I detoured to the university store to pick one up. By the time I got back to my room, my required reading rate had jumped to nineteen pages an hour.

Four hours later, I finished my first thirty-page chapter, driving my forward-rate up further to 20.625. It was my practice to review reading assignments immediately upon completion by browsing those parts of the chapter I had highlighted in yellow. I typically highlighted the first paragraph of each section and then the topic sentence of each ensuing paragraph and anything else that seemed important.

Upon review, in a striking forerunner of the "All work and no play makes Jack a dull boy" scene from Stanley Kubrick's *The Shining*, I discovered that I had highlighted every line in the chapter.

Anyway, that's where the dream always ends. The great

The B-Side of Paradise

Math 447 dream of my life. That has been calling me back—like that waitress from the Princetonian Diner —for the past forty-three years. The lesson, as there always must be one, is simple:

Princeton never forgets. And you won't, either.

Beckett's Best-Fit College Search

What's most revealing about my Math 447 dream is when I stopped having it. Which was only a few short years ago, coincident with my son Beckett's college search.

I should have known that naming our second born after the tragicomic playwright whose master work, *Endgame,* was about a man who kept his parents stashed away in garbage cans, would come back to haunt me some day. Still, who could have imagined how closely the spirit of the man who once said, "Every word is like an unnecessary stain on silence and nothingness," would live on in my son?

Beckett's college counselor gave me an apt demonstration of how kindred the boy's spirit was with his namesake when he called to read me his verbatim responses to the student profile prompts he had given him that day. They were: "I don't know." "I'm not sure." "I never thought about it." "Maybe." And "Something." "Something" being his answer to the prompt, "What do you think you would like to major in?"

"That sounds like Beckett," I said, not sure anymore if I

was referring to my son or the playwright. Then he asked if I could share any insights about him that he could work with.

"I don't know," I said. "He doesn't talk to me, either."

"Well, you see him around the house."

"Not really, he stays in his room a lot."

That night at dinner, my wife and I had a chat with Beckett about his college plans. I suspected he was interested in the University of Pennsylvania because a dashing redheaded friend of his was a student there. I suggested we drive down that weekend and take a tour. "We could head down to DC after Penn and check out Georgetown."

He turned to my wife and asked, "What about..." Then he nodded his head sideways in my direction and pointed a forkful of homemade Moroccan chickpea stew my way for emphasis. Which I correctly interpreted as "What about dad?" "What about dad's school?" "What about Princeton?"

The prospect of his applying to Princeton had never crossed my mind. I always assumed that after my performance, the university would not be inclined to double down on another generation of the Flying Cannoli family from Baytown. Somewhere deep in the bowels of the admissions office on University Place, I imagined there is a file with my name on it and a big red "No Legacy" stamp over it. Lest the institutional record otherwise fail to note my association with any of the legendary "eventful evenings" mentioned in this book.

It's amazing how quickly a taciturn teen who can go weeks without verbal communications beyond "idk" and an occasional "wtf" can transform into Ivy admissions gold in a parent's eyes. But the fact of the matter was that he had nosebleed grades, was an accomplished musician on three instruments, and a track star. More importantly, he was nothing like me. But a lot like the other people who go to Princeton.

Beckett's Best-Fit College Search

I found myself saying in an uncharacteristically grown-up voice "Well, you certainly would be a viable candidate at Princeton. If you're serious, we can work in a tour there, as well." So, we piled into the car much as an earlier generation of my family had done on the day of the ACC Abortion, and drove down to Princeton, Penn, and Georgetown.

After our Princeton visit, my wife suggested Beckett develop a pro and con list for each of the schools we saw that weekend. Princeton got mixed reviews. Beckett liked the Henry Moore sculpture *Oval with Points*—even before I told him you could sit in it. Whereupon he conceded that that would make it "cooler, still." He also liked that you could take a bus or train into New York City right from campus. And the breakfast quesadilla at PJ's Pancake House.

On the con side, he insisted on calling Nassau Hall's famous two-story faculty room with its British House of Commons seating "The Tomb." He said the info session we attended in it under the watchful eyes of George Washington and King George II was, "idk, creepy." And he thought our tour guide, who wore beige knee socks and spoke perhaps too at-length about her study abroad cheese-making workshop in Provence, was, "idk, boring."

But he couldn't get a handle on Penn at all. And he said Georgetown was, "idk, sketchy." Which put Princeton firmly back in play, I thought. I could see all the dominoes falling now. Beckett would come around, without any undue parental influence, to the now obvious in my mind conclusion that Princeton was his Best-Fit School after all.

He would write his application essay about *The Six*, the Superhero film he made for AB Calc that demonstrated all twelve principles of calculus he learned in the class and paid faithful tribute to the classic *SpongeBob SquarePants* episode

"Karate Island." It couldn't fail but to make him an ED1 shoo-in, and my legacy would live on.

I could almost taste the sugary maple syrup on the buckwheat pancakes at PJ's Pancake House when we dropped him off for Orientation Week in the fall. Until it all came crashing down for my alma mater on the grassy academic quad of Tufts University in Medford, Massachusetts, just one week later.

The trouble began when a virile, long-haired crew jock and self-described math geek announced he would be our tour guide. He had a funny way of putting things that Beckett could relate to. Like when he said, "Tufts is the kind of place where people are not afraid to just geek out in public."

If that line wasn't Beckett's deciding factor in his college choice, then the tour guide's funny socks with math symbols on them surely were. Because my son also had funny socks with math symbols on them that he would wear to track practice on Funny Sock Wednesdays. When I saw the nth root radical symbol in Day-Glo green on the tour guide's socks, I knew Princeton was toast.

In this manner, for the second time in as many generations, my road-tripping-challenged family offered up an object lesson on the futility of rational college decision-making. And that little round laughing man in my head went off again.

We tried to explain the importance of applying to a breadth of safety, expected, and reach schools. But Beckett refused to apply anywhere but Tufts. He assured us that if his early decision application didn't go the right way on December 1, he would reconsider his options at that time.

And with that, my legacy died. Along with my Math 447 dream. As if only when the Flying Cannoli threat was safely removed, would Princeton finally let me have some peace.

A Cold Pony To Go

A year later, I dusted off my notes and started writing *The B-Side of Paradise*. Imagine my surprise when I discovered my real college career wasn't nearly as triumphant as the one, I had been carrying around in my head for the past 43 years. I didn't win the Pyne Prize, make All Ivy or marry the college president's daughter. And it was a sobering moment when it hit me that: surrounded by the entire history of human thought for four years, the only ideas that truly piqued my interest… were my own.

Still, some might say, "kudos" for finally getting around to inking the stories I was pissing and moaning about with the registrar that day in my senior year. Others will take a dim view of my procrastination. But patience can be a virtue, as it was revealed to me, only with the aid of the space of time, that the most disturbing consequence of graduating from Princeton was that I couldn't take my college friends with me.

And I realized that I've spent all my days since searching for them—or somebody like them—in every crowd, on every train, around every corner. Just as I did for Haiku

The B-Side of Paradise

George, Firesign Doug, and "what's all this hoo-ha about marijuana" Charlie my first day on campus. Now, in a way, I have brought them back into my life. Like Daisy's green light, Gatsby's future receding into his past. To raise a cold pony to the heterodox and the holy who joined me, if ever so briefly, for a front row seat on *The B-Side of Paradise*.

Especially those who are no longer with us. May they rest in peace. Pablo, my football confidante. The backgammon master Gio. Gentleman Jack Bourbon. Ersatz Cowboy Joel. And the sassy to her grave Strong Confident Woman.

This book is going to be tough to explain to my kids.